Pilgrim's Problems

Other books by Karl Haffner

Pilgrim's Problems

Turn your troubles into triumphs
on the road to God's front door

KARL HAFFNER

Pacific Press® Publishing Association
Nampa, Idaho
Oshawa, Ontario, Canada
www.pacificpress.com

Edited by Chelsey Ham
Designed by Dennis Ferree
Cover illustration by Pearl Beach

Additional copies of this book are available by calling toll free 1-800-765-6955 or
visiting http://www.adventistbookcenter.com.

Library of Congress Cataloging-in-Publication-Data

Haffner, Karl, 1961–
Pilgrim's Problems : turn your troubles into triumphs on the road to
God's front door/Karl Haffner.
p. cm.
Includes bibliographical references.
ISBN: 0-8163-2022-5
1. Christian life—Meditations. I. Title.

BV4501.3.H345 2004
248.4'867—dc22   2003068996

04 05 06 07 08 • 5 4 3 2 1

Dedication

Once in a great while, God plops people in our lives who redefine the meaning of supportive. For me, this family is the Melashenko and Wallace tribe.

Bob, Connie, George, and Dana, thank you for your encouragement through the years. I treasure your friendship. I love your choice of restaurants. I laugh at your stories. I marvel at your generous hearts. I remember the wedding fondly. I aspire to be the kind of cheerleader for others that you have been for me. I wish you God's best always. I miss seeing you regularly. And I dedicate this book to you.

Mucho thanks to my favorite . . .

Sanitation engineer, Tim Lale, for cleaning up the messy manuscripts I send him.

Delusionist, Rhett Unger, for reminding me that it's better to be delusional and happy than realistic and depressed.

Palm Pilot Debbie Johnson for organizing my scattered life.

Little buddy, Andy Litchfield, for inviting me into his circle of trust.

Comfort-food connoisseurs, Jerry and Lisa Bryant, for reminding me that life without fun is, well, ... no fun.

Teammates, Henning, John, Leslie, Troy, Lois, and Lana, for being "eminently doable" kind of thinkers.

Smile-makers, Lindsey and Claire, for being the best kids a daddy could ever hope for.

Folks, Mom and Dad, for always being there since my drooling days.

Best friend, Cherié, for sharing a life with me.

Contents

Introduction

"Condemn the fault, and not the actor of it."
—WILLIAM SHAKESPEARE

Some years ago, after I spoke at a religious conference, a gentleman handed me a note on his way out of the auditorium.

"Thank you!" I said.

He scowled. His face was so sour he probably could have sucked buttons off a sofa. Then he barked, "Sonny, you may want to read that letter before you say 'thank you.'"

"Oh, OK! It's one of *those* letters!" I smirked.

So later that year (I wasn't really anxious to get to it) I tore into it. Sure enough, it wasn't a merry missive. While I can't remember exactly what the missile said (Why keep hate mail?), I do recall one of his gripes centered on my choice of illustrations. He felt strongly that pastors should never disclose their own struggles and shortcomings. He was offended that I should tell of the time my wife, Cherié, and I had an argument or when I lost my cool in a traffic altercation. As he put it, "I don't want to see the pastor's pimples." He was implying, of course, that preachers ought to cake on enough makeup that we don't look real. The rationale is that it's better to be dishonest and look holy than to be honest about our imperfect holiness.

Well, guess what? Pilgrims have problems too. Even saints struggle with sin. Mind you, preachers are not always up front about this. We're

Introduction

masters at posturing ourselves as the squeakiest of the clean. Listen carefully and you'll notice how often preachers tell stories that put them in the best possible light.

For example, ever hear a preacher refer to a TV show by saying, "I was just flipping through the channels the other day and I happened to see . . ."? The disclaimer is subtle but meant to be noticed: "I don't watch much TV. I just so happened to have twenty-six seconds between seventeen Bible studies and thirteen baptisms when I tuned in and saw . . ."

---

*T*here is so much good in the worst of us,
And so much bad in the best of us,
That it hardly behooves any of us
To talk about the rest of us.
—EDWARD WALLIS HOCH

Well, the truth about this preacher is that sometimes I sit down and watch TV. Bag of Cheetos snacks in the left hand, bowl of Ben and Jerry's Chunky Monkey ice cream in the right—and I'm not flipping channels. Nor am I watching 3ABN; sometimes I camp on FOX.

As recently as last night I was flipping through the channels (really!) and heard a TV preacher tell a story of eating pizza with his son. He began the story with this qualifier: "I haven't had pizza in two years, but to be with my boy I compromised my health standards and . . ."

Why the need to explain how long it had been since the last slice of pleasure? Like most pilgrims he wanted to preserve an appearance of perfection. But, of course, we all know it's bunk. Truth is, no one's perfect.

If you can accept that truth, then you're ready to sign on for this journey through the pages of Scripture that inform us on how to triumph over troubles like loneliness, resentment, pride, and guilt. That's what this book is all about.

PILGRIM'S PROBLEMS

God's most-honored dead

Our first step in this journey begins with a tour through God's Westminster Abbey. In London, there's a giant, thousand-year-old cathedral called Westminster Abbey, built in the form of a cross. It has been the setting for every coronation since 1066 and for numerous other royal occasions. It still functions as a church dedicated to regular worship and to the celebration of great events in the life of the nation. It is also where England buries her most-honored dead: kings, statesmen, soldiers, scientists, poets, musicians, and scholars. The elite get buried in the Abbey.

In a sense, God has a Westminster Abbey too. It's located in Hebrews chapter 11. That's where you'll find the saints whom God would honor most. Who gets this special burial? Do you suppose it's limited to pilgrims without problems? Let's take a look.

Now faith is being sure of what we hope for and certain of what we do not see. This is what the ancients were commended for.

By faith we understand that the universe was formed at God's command, so that what is seen was not made out of what was visible.

By faith Abel offered God a better sacrifice than Cain did. By faith he was commended as a righteous man, when God spoke well of his offerings. And by faith he still speaks, even though he is dead.[1]

No surprises yet. Abel is the first pilgrim to make God's honor roll. He was, after all, the first martyr. We read on:

By faith Enoch was taken from this life, so that he did not experience death; he could not be found, because God had taken him away. For before he was taken, he was commended as one who pleased God. And without faith it is impossible to please God, because anyone who comes to him must believe that he exists and that he rewards those who earnestly seek him.[2]

Introduction

Again, it's no surprise to find Enoch among God's most-honored dead. Remember that he walked with God.

But now our tour takes an odd twist. "By faith Noah, when warned about things not yet seen, in holy fear built an ark to save his family. By his faith he condemned the world and became heir of the righteousness that comes by faith."[3]

No man is perfect unless he admits his faults. But if he has faults to admit, how can he be perfect?
—Anonymous

Excuse me, but did I hear Noah included among God's most-honored dead? Isn't that the same guy who celebrated the end of the Flood by getting drunk? How much confidence would you have in an evangelist who blew into your church and celebrated a successful series by getting plastered? Yet God must consider Noah to be special. After all, he's buried with the most-honored dead.

Now get a load of this next guy.

By faith Abraham, when called to go to a place he would later receive as his inheritance, obeyed and went, even though he did not know where he was going. By faith he made his home in the Promised Land like a stranger in a foreign country; he lived in tents, as did Isaac and Jacob, who were heirs with him of the same promise. For he was looking forward to the city with foundations, whose architect and builder is God. By faith Abraham, even though he was past age—and Sarah herself was barren—was enabled to become a father because he considered him faithful who had made the promise. And so from this one man, and he as good as dead, came descendants as numerous as the stars in the sky and as countless as the sand on the seashore.[4]

PILGRIM'S PROBLEMS

Why would Abraham get a five-verse plaque posted in his honor? He's the spiritual *schmuck* who lied to the government at the price of his wife's chastity. He got booted out of the country. That's worse than cheating on your income tax!

It only gets worse!

> By faith Moses' parents hid him for three months after he was born, because they saw he was no ordinary child, and they were not afraid of the king's edict. By faith Moses, when he had grown up, refused to be known as the son of Pharaoh's daughter. He chose to be mistreated along with the people of God rather than to enjoy the pleasures of sin for a short time. He regarded disgrace for the sake of Christ as of greater value than the treasures of Egypt, because he was looking ahead to his reward. By faith he left Egypt, not fearing the king's anger; he persevered because he saw him who is invisible. By faith he kept the Passover and the sprinkling of blood, so that the destroyer of the firstborn would not touch the firstborn of Israel. By faith the people passed through the Red Sea as on dry land; but when the Egyptians tried to do so, they were drowned.[5]

---

*As you receive the Spirit of Christ—
the Spirit of unselfish love and labor
for others—you will grow and
bring forth fruit. The graces of the Spirit
will ripen in your character. Your faith
will increase, your convictions deepen,
your love be made perfect. More and more
you will reflect the likeness of Christ in all
that is pure, noble, and lovely.*
—ELLEN WHITE, *CHRIST'S OBJECT LESSONS, 67*

All this flattery for a murderer—give me a break.

Introduction

And we could go on. Next we see Rahab, the prostitute. Then comes Samson, the chap who needed Dr. Laura, Dr. Phil, Dr. Ruth, and Dr. Seuss—any doctor! And let's not forget David; he's included among God's most-honored dead. He was not only an adulterer but a murderer (and to think he did all this while he was General Conference president!).

Take-homes from the tour

You can learn a lot in museums—and this one is no exception. Of the many take-homes we could dig from this chapter, let me highlight three.

1. In our weakness, we are made strong.

In verse 34 the author wants us to know that a common thread weaving through all the sordid stories of the saints is that their "weakness was turned to strength."

Recently I heard the story of a ten-year-old boy who took up the sport of judo—despite the fact that he had lost his left arm in a car accident. The boy signed on to study under an old Japanese judo master. Although the boy was making great progress, he felt frustrated because, after three months of training, the master had taught him only one move.

"Sensei," the boy respectfully protested, "why can't I learn some other moves?"

"Keep perfecting this move. It is the most important one," the sensei replied.

Not fully understanding, but fully trusting the teacher, the boy kept training. After several months he was ready for his first competition.

Surprising himself, the boy easily won his first two matches and advanced to the semi-finals. The next match proved to be more difficult, but after some time, his opponent became restless and charged. The boy deftly used his one move to score a victory.

Stunned by his unexpected success, the boy was now in the finals. This time, his opponent was quicker, stronger, and more experienced. For most of the match the boy seemed to be outplayed. Worried about the boy's safety, the referee tried to call the match. "No!" the sensei insisted. "Let the match continue. My boy is still in it."

Shortly thereafter, the boy's opponent dropped his guard. Instantly the boy used his one move to pin him. Thus, the boy left with the first-place trophy that stood nearly as tall as he did!

On the ride home, the boy and the sensei discussed every move of each match. Then the boy asked the burning question: "Sensei, how did I win the tournament when I really only knew one move?"

"You won for two reasons. First, you've almost mastered one of the most challenging throws in judo. And second, the only known defense for that move is for your opponent to grab your left arm." The boy's biggest weakness had become his biggest strength.

---

*We have a bat's eyes
for our own faults, and an eagle's
for the faults of others.*
—James L. Gordon

Remember that story the next time you're inclined to beat yourself up because of your flaws. Truth is, you're a perfect collage of strengths and weaknesses. Embrace them both. For God can work through you even when you feel inadequate; or better yet, *especially* when you feel inadequate.

The apostle Paul once wrote this: "I quit focusing on [my] handicap.... Now I take limitations in stride, and with good cheer, these limitations that cut me down to size—abuse, accidents, opposition, bad breaks. I just let Christ take over! And so the weaker I get, the stronger I become."[6] In our weakness we are made strong.

2. In our trials, we are called to faith.

In verse 39 of Hebrews 11 we find another common compliment that applies to all the imperfect pilgrims. After a graphic description in verses 34–38 of the horrendous trials that these saints endured, the author tells us: "These were all commended for their faith." Why did all these people land in God's Westminster Abbey? Because in their trials, they demonstrated great faith.

One of my favorite stories of faith is that of ABC news correspondent Josh Howell. He's the man who held an apple for Olympic gold medalist, Darrel Pace. The demonstration was the headliner at an archery exhibition in New York City's Central Park. Shooting steel-tipped hunting arrows, Pace punctured many bull's-eyes without a miss.

Then he called for a volunteer. "All you have to do," said Pace, "is hold this apple in your hand, waist-high." Josh Howell took a bold step forward. As he stood there, a small apple in his hand, a larger one in his throat, Pace took aim from thirty yards away as the audience gawked.

Then *thwack!* Pace launched a clean hit that exploded the apple before striking the target behind. Everybody applauded Howell, who was all smiles—until his cameraman approached with a hound-dog look. "I'm sorry, Josh," he said. "I didn't get it. Had a problem with my viewfinder. Could you do it again?"[7]

3. In our faith, we are made perfect.

Notice how this chapter ends: "These were all commended for their faith . . . God had planned something better for us so that only together with us would they be made perfect."[8]

Notice, God assumes the responsibility to make us perfect. God's plan for His people is that they would be "made perfect." Too often we grit our teeth and try our hardest to be perfect. But it's very frustrating. God says, "That's My job. I'll assume responsibility to change you."

What, then, is our responsibility?

We must exercise faith. We have to trust God to change us. The battle is not in trying to stop sinning. The battle is in trying to keep trusting. God does the changing. We do the trusting.

The children's book *Little Lord Fauntleroy* tells the story of a seven-year-old boy who went to stay with his grandpa. Although the man had a reputation of being extremely mean and selfish, the lad took a great interest in him. Over and over the boy complimented his grandpa, finding only positive things to say about him.

"Oh, Grandpa," he gushed, "how people must love you! You're so good and kind in all you do." No matter how disagreeable the elderly man was, the grandson saw the best in everything Grandpa did.

Finally, the youngster's unquestioning love softened the heart of the cantankerous old man. Grandpa couldn't resist the unwavering trust that the boy had in his goodness. As a result, he gradually began to change his ways, and in time he became the unselfish and kind person his grandson thought him to be.

Although it's just a make-believe kid's tale, it does capture the true story of us all. Like Grandpa, you and I *can* change. We can become unselfish and kind—just like Jesus! Now mind you, this change doesn't occur by trying hard to change. That's as fruitless and frustrating as trying to get a tan in a dark room by gritting your teeth and clenching your fists and chanting, "I will get a sun tan! I will get a sun tan!"

How often do we try to change and fight temptation by that method of trying really hard to be perfect? "I will not take a drink; I will not gossip; I will not eat that pie; I will not . . ." It's much simpler. To tan, live in the sun.

Similarly, to overcome sin, live in the Son. Don't waste your time trying to be holy. Instead, live in the presence of He who is holy. Then, as you live in the Son, you'll change. He will make you perfect in His righteousness.

Ellen White puts it like this: "Christ died for us, making full and abundant provision for our redemption. Although by our disobedience we have merited God's displeasure and condemnation, He has not forsaken us; He has not left us to grapple with the power of the enemy in our own finite strength. Heavenly angels fight our battles for us; and co-operating with them, we may be victorious over the powers of evil. Trusting in Christ as our personal Savior, we may be 'more than conquerors through him that loved us' (Rom. 8:37)."[9] It really is possible to prevail over our problems—but this does not happen in our own power. We are conquerors by trusting in Christ.

Now let's put some skin on this concept of faith and consider what it looks like in real life. In 1930 on an island in the Philippines, a man name Frank Laubach climbed to the top of Signal Hill. He felt crushed by a sense of disappointment with his life. His

Introduction

career was a failure in his eyes. He had hoped to be president of a college. He almost had the opportunity, but out of chivalry he voted for his opponent and lost the position by one vote. Three of Laubach's children died of malaria. Because of health hazards, his wife and remaining child lived 900 miles away. The people he was trying to help rejected him. God seemed very far away. Although a student of the finest theological education available, Laubach thought of Jesus as a good man who lived a long time ago, but nothing more.

In despair, he sat on the summit and tried to talk to God. That's when something very mysterious happened to him. His belief—and you can decide for yourself what you think—was that God began to speak to him.

God invited him to do an experiment with the rest of his life—to devote himself to living and walking with God. The target was to make each hour a continual, inner conversation with God and to be perfectly responsive to His will.

*If the best man's faults
were written on his forehead,
he would draw his hat over his eyes.*
—THOMAS GRAY

For the next forty years, that's what Frank Laubach did. He wrote this:

The most wonderful discovery that has ever come to me is that I do not have to wait until some future time for the glorious hour. I need not sing, "Oh that will be glory for me—" and wait for any grave. *This hour* can be heaven. *Any* hour for *any* body can be as rich as God! For do you not see that God is trying experiments with human lives. That is why there are so many of them. He has one billion seven hundred million experiments going around the world at this moment. And His question is, "How far will this man and that woman allow me to carry this hour?"[10]

How far? Frank Laubach devoted his life to this one question. He got very practical, using images, props, notes, Scripture, pictures, sounds, and anything else to remind himself to live in the presence of God. In his books he outlined dozens of ways that he would try to help his mind, minute by minute, realize that God was with him all through the day.

Far from making himself into a hermit, this partnership with God thrust Laubach back into the world and made him into an unbelievable blessing for others. He believed the acid test of true spiritual life is that it leads you to feed the hungry, visit the sick, give where there's poverty, serve where there's need.

That's what happened to him. He became the leader of the worldwide literacy movement. (The phrase, "Each one, teach one" originated with him.) He became an advisor to U.S. presidents. He was also one of the primary shapers of U.S. foreign policy after WWII—especially the Marshall plan that rebuilt cities out of ashes.

Frank Laubach's secret was simple: He learned to walk with God. He put feet to his faith so that every moment was an experiment in trusting Jesus. He lived simply, deeply, continuously, one day at a time in conversation with Christ. Like Enoch, he walked with God.

If God were inducting modern-day saints into His Westminster Abbey, no doubt Frank Laubach would have a plaque in his honor.

For in his weakness, he was made strong. In his trials, he was called to faith. In his faith, he was made perfect. Frank Laubach discovered the perfection of Jesus—residing moment by moment in Him.

You, too, can enter into this adventure. How? By faith.

BRINGING IT HOME

Who do I think would be included in God's Westminster Abbey today? Why?

Introduction

What step of faith is God asking me to take right now?

What weaknesses do I have that God might use as my strengths?

How can I use my trials to build faith?

Devise a personal plan to practice Laubach's technique of living every minute in the presence of Jesus. Take a risk today that requires reckless faith in God. Write a letter to God confessing your imperfections. Ask Him to change you from the inside out.

[1] Hebrews 11:1-4.

[2] Hebrews 11:5, 6.

[3] Hebrews 11:7.

[4] Hebrews 11:8-12.

[5] Hebrews 11:23-29.

[6] 2 Corinthians 12:9, 10, *The Message.*

[7] Adapted from Bob Teague, *Live and Off-Color: News Biz* as found on Web site: <http://www.christianglobe.com/Illustrations/theDetails.asp?whichOne=f&whichFile=faith>

[8] Hebrews 11:39, 40.

[9] Ellen White, *God's Amazing Grace,* 1973, p. 10.

[10] Frank Laubach, *Letters By A Modern Mystic, Excerpts from letters written at Dansalan, Lake Lanao, Philippine Islands,* as quoted at <http:// durrance.com/laubach.htm>.

If you have made mistakes, even serious mistakes, there is always another chance for you. And supposing you have tried and failed again and again, you may have a fresh start any moment you choose, for this thing that we call "failure" is not the falling down, but the staying down.

—MARY PICKFORD

CHAPTER ONE

Failure

"A failure, within God's purpose, is no longer really a failure. Thus the cross, the Supreme Failure, is at the same time the Supreme Triumph of God, since it is the accomplishment of the purpose of salvation."
—PAUL TOURNIER

Two bums were leaning against a tree in the fields. One said, "I'm sick and tired of this life. I'm sick and tired of sleeping in the cold and rain, begging for food, wearing torn clothes. I'm sick of it."

The second bum said, "If you feel like that, why don't you get a job?"

The first bum sat up and said, "And admit I'm a failure?"

Generally speaking, we're not big on admitting failure. Even though we've all been bummed out by that feeling, right? Failure is that familiar feeling of saying something you regret, of compromising your integrity, of caving in to the same old sin, of being paralyzed by lurid thoughts, of snubbing God—again.

And whether you care to admit it or not, failure is a part of your spiritual portfolio. Every pilgrim's got a problem on this one. But don't despair. Consider Karen Mains's take on failure:

> Nature shouts of this beginning-again-God, this God who can make all our failures regenerative, the One who is God of risings again, who never tires of fresh starts, nativities, renaissances in persons or in culture. God is a God of starting over, of genesis and re-genesis. He composts life's sour fruits, moldering rank and decomposing; He applies the organic matter to

our new day chances; He freshens the world with dew; He hydrates withered human hearts with his downpouring spirit.[1]

The psalmist put it like this: "My flesh and my heart may fail, but God is the strength of my heart and my portion forever."[2] The author of Lamentations adds, "Because of the Lord's great love we are not consumed, for his compassions never fail. They are new every morning; great is your faithfulness."[3]

No matter the magnitude of your failure, you can begin again. This truth sings from the story of Jacques Celliers. Since stories tend to be our strongest teachers, we'll devote the remainder of this chapter to one story. Let's begin with the tragic end of his story.

Jacques Celliers died in Java, at a prisoner-of-war camp just before peace was declared in 1945. In gross violation of camp rules, an irate Japanese officer was poised to execute one of the prisoners. In an attempt to save his friend's life, Celliers approached the Japanese officer and kissed him on both cheeks like a French general honoring a soldier after a decoration for valor. The shock and humiliation of this gesture so infuriated the officer that he had Celliers killed instead.

Reconciliation is not weakness or cowardice. It demands courage, nobility, generosity, sometimes heroism, an overcoming of oneself rather than of one's adversary.
—POPE PAUL VI

The manner of Celliers's death was disturbingly inhumane. The prisoners were ordered to dig a hole in the center of the compound. Celliers was then escorted out of his cell and dumped into the hole. His comrades were then forced to fill the hole, leaving exposed only Celliers's bruised head. Two days later, his strikingly handsome face and sun-bleached hair slumped into the dirt.

Before he died, however, Celliers recorded his life story. Wrapping his journal in a piece of military ground cloth, he buried it in

Failure

the cell floor where it was later discovered. In it, the story of Celliers's triumph over failure is preserved. It begins with these sobering words:

> I had a brother once and I betrayed him. The betrayal in itself was so slight that most people would find "betrayal" too exaggerated a word, and think me morbidly sensitive for so naming it. Yet as one recognizes the nature of the seed from the tree, the tree by its fruit, and the fruit from the taste on the tongue, so I know the betrayal from its consequences and the tyrannical flavour it left behind it in my emotions.[4]

Celliers was the oldest of four children—two girls, two boys. Both of the girls died in the typhoid epidemic that ravaged their homeland of South Africa. Thus only the two boys remained.

There could not be a sharper contrast between Celliers and his brother. Celliers was tall, strong, and incredibly handsome. His skin was flawless, his face punctuated by dark blue eyes and crowned in flowing blond hair. Stories flourished of times when Celliers would walk into a crowded room and people would cease their conversations to stare. Celliers was a natural leader with a keen intellect, a sharp tongue, and natural athletic abilities. He fostered a deep love for the outdoors, often roaming the bushveldt of South Africa to observe the majestic animals. It was clear that destiny had smiled upon him at birth.

His brother, seven years his junior, was different in every possible way. He was short, awkward, poor at academics, and as athletic as a platypus wearing ice skates. His hair was thick and dark and grew menacingly low onto his forehead. His skin was Mediterranean olive. His eyes burned of an intense radiant blackness, which prompted Celliers to later recount, "I could never look in them without feeling curiously disturbed and uncomfortable." Celliers also added, "I wish I could deal more firmly with this subtle discomfort but I cannot. I only know it was there from the beginning and as far back as I can remember it expressed itself from time to time in an involuntary feeling of irritation which, no matter how unreasonable and unfair, no matter what precautions I took to the contrary, would break out im-

PILGRIM'S PROBLEMS

patiently from me."[5] He cared little for animals but loved to work in dirt. Whatever he planted seemed to grow.

There was one area, however, where genetics had flipped the coin. Celliers was tone deaf. In contrast, from an early age the younger brother had a clear, unhesitating soprano voice which developed as he grew older into a manly and perfectly pure tenor instrument. He even composed music that moved the deepest emotions. Celliers recalled a signature tune that always stirred his innermost, unrealized longings. The lyrics went like this:

> Ride, ride through the day,
> Ride through the moonlight
> Ride, ride through the night.
> For far in the distance burns your fire
> For someone who has waited long.

But there was one irregularity, more than any other that blighted that brother's life. Between his shoulders grew a razor-edged hump. It brought him such shame that he never spoke of it. His mother padded his jackets to try and camouflage that awful projection. Although it was actually nothing more than a slight deformity, it grew like a mountain in his mind, making him a recluse from the world. In his journal Celliers recounts, "We never referred to it by name. We always designated it by an atmospheric blank in our sentences. For instance, I would say, 'But if you do go swimming there wouldn't they see…blank.' Or he to me: 'D'you think if I wore that linen jacket it would…blank…you know?' "[6]

That hump is what prompted Celliers to begin his story with the confession, "I had a brother once and I betrayed him." The torment of his failure dated back to his senior year in school. Halfway through that last year, Celliers' parents decided to send his brother to join him at boarding school. Although the brother needed another year at the village school, the parents thought it would be easier for him if he had an older brother to guide his awkward paces that first year away from home.

The year had gone well for Celliers. He recalls,

I was in the first eleven, captained the first fifteen, won the

Failure

Victor Lodorum medal at the annual inter-school athletics, and was first in my final form. ... Both masters and boys confidently predicted that at the close of the year I would be awarded the most coveted prize of the school, that for the best all-round man of the year. It was to this brilliant and crowded stage that I returned from vacation with my strange brother at my side.[7]

Little did Celliers anticipate how quickly the students would spread the news of this "strange fish" that had been thrown up on the school beach when his brother arrived. Celliers recalls, "From the very first evening, the start was not encouraging. First impressions are important to the young and never more important than when there are initiation rites to perform."[8]

---

*F*orgiveness is the fragrance
that the flower leaves on the heel
of the one who crushed it.
—MARK TWAIN

Celliers had discussed the initiation proceedings on numerous occasions with his brother. He told him about running the gauntlet in pajamas with the students standing in two rows flicking wet towels plaited to a fine lashlike point; about waking up at night and finding a boy sitting with pillows on his head while others put a slip-knot of a fishing line round his toes and pulled at them until they bled in a perfect circle; about being made to measure the distance from school to town with his toothbrush on the holidays. As Celliers described the type of initiations that could transpire, nothing seemed to dismay the brother. The only thing he truly feared was his back being exposed and ridiculed.

On numerous occasions Celliers responded to his brother's big question: "You don't suppose they would make fun of ... you know ... will they?"

"Of course not," Celliers replied. "You're going to a decent school, not a calf pen."[9]

In spite of Celliers's emphatic answer, his brother worried constantly about being exposed. Over and over Celliers heard the same question: "They won't—will they?"

One evening Celliers snapped. "Won't what? Never ask me again! Do you understand?"

The question was on his brother's lips again as Celliers conducted rounds of the dormitories the night before the initiations were to take place. Noticing his brother's apprehension, Celliers turned quickly away and bade him a curt "good night" before slamming the door.

After rounds Celliers joined the head monitors of the other three dorms in the office of the captain of the school. Following the usual pleasantries, the captain said, "We need to talk about the little matter of tomorrow's initiation. I take it you've all interviewed the newcomers in your houses. Have you any youngster you think should be excused?"

"Yes," the young man next to Celliers replied. "I have a boy with a weak heart who brought a doctor's certificate."

"No problem," the captain replied.

"Yes," said another, "I have a boy who is blind as a bat. He'd probably better be excused all the physical rites though there is no reason why he shouldn't be available for the rest of the fun."

After a couple other students were mentioned, the captain looked keenly at Celliers. "No one?" the captain asked.

"No," Celliers said.

"You've got a young brother in your house, haven't you?" the captain asked.

"I have."

"What about him?"

"Well, what about him?" Celliers sparred.

"I was merely wondering if he was all right—"

"Of course he's all right." Celliers's answer was vehement; still the captain persisted.

"Forgive me, old chap," he said. "I don't want to badger you. If you say he's all right we all accept it. But, knowing you, we realize the last thing you'd ask for would be special dispensation for a relative. So if you've any reason for wanting your brother excused tomorrow we'd none of us think of it as favouritism."

Spontaneous agreement was expressed around the table. But Celliers insisted, "Awfully decent of you but there's no reason, honestly."

The following day after classes, Celliers hid in the distance as he spied on his brother standing by the door of the senior science laboratory. He stood tentative, as he always did when possessed by only one thought.

Suddenly a stampede of unruly students appeared. They hoisted the Celliers kid on their shoulders and started chanting, "Why was he born so beautiful, why was he born at all?" The mob grew rowdier and rowdier until one of the bigger boys shouted, "Chaps, this new-comer has got to do something for our entertainment. What shall it be?"

"Make him sing," a voice from the mob replied.

"Right!" the student punched him with a fist on the shoulder and demanded, "Come on, Greenie, you've had your orders. Sing, blast you, sing!"

Celliers remembers it like this:

Music as I have told you was peculiarly my brother's own idiom. With the prospect of singing, even in such circumstances, his courage appeared to come back. He obeyed at once and began to sing:
Ride, ride through the day,
Ride through the moonlight
Ride, ride through the night.
For far in the distance burns the fire
For someone who has waited long.
The opening notes were perhaps a trifle uncertain but before the end of the first line his gift for music confidently took over. By the second line his little tune sounded well and truly launched. But he didn't realize, poor devil, that the very faultlessness of his performance was the worst thing that could have happened. ... The boys, quick to feel that the clear voice singing with such unusual authority was cheating the design of its ritual uttered an extraordinary howl of disapproval.[10]

PILGRIM'S PROBLEMS

The gang began to press toward a long, deep horse trough chanting, "Greenie's a liar and a cheat, He can't sing a note. Greenie's a fraud: drown him, drown him in the moat!"[11]

Celliers remembers what happened next:

> For a moment my brother's white face remained outlined against the afternoon fire flaming along the red-brick quadrangle wall, his eyes ceaselessly searching the screaming, whistling mob of schoolboys. Then he vanished like the last shred of sail of a doomed ship into a grasping sea. ... I could not see what was happening. My experience told me that my brother was being ducked vigorously in the trough as we had all been before him. I knew the "drown" in the chant really meant "duck." All the same I was extremely nervous. I watched the struggle and tumult of yelling heads and shoulders by the water-trough, wondering whether it would never end.[12]

Instantly the crowed went motionless and silent. An arm shot up holding a shirt and behind it a naked torso.

Those who experience soul hunger are to be blessed with satisfaction. Their earnest, prayerful struggles will not be in vain; for there is no failure with God. For all our imperfections there is forgiveness with God.

—ELLEN WHITE, SIGNS OF THE TIMES,
SEPTEMBER 5, 1895

"Look, chaps!" a voice rang out with a curious reflection. "Greenie has a humpback!"

For a moment there was silence as the boys stared at the dripping wet hump. Then they exploded with laughter, twisting and turning in hysterics.

Failure

In that moment of terror, a teacher burst onto the scene and squelched the madness. But peace came too late and at too high a cost. That young, vulnerable, awkward boy was scarred for life. After the revealing of his ugly scar, he dropped out of school.

Celliers remembered and lamented in his prison cell, "I had a brother once and I betrayed him." Celliers felt overwhelmed by his failure. The brothers rarely spoke again after the incident. A door on brotherhood had been slammed so tightly shut that neither of the two boys could pry it open.

The young brother went home to his garden and solitude and never sang a note. Celliers graduated and became a successful lawyer, but his heart was empty.

At the outbreak of World War II, Celliers was one of the first to volunteer. Although he was recruited for an administrative post in the Adjutant-General's department, Celliers insisted that he be commissioned in the infantry instead. Getting his wish, he was soon sent with the first division of infantry to the battlefields of North Africa. There, the great need was for a special patrol to capture enemy soldiers to provide them information. Celliers volunteered to carry out this dangerous mission and penetrate deep behind enemy lines. In this military maneuver Celliers found his niche. Coupled with his lifetime's experience in stalking game in his native land, Celliers was uniquely gifted for this task, thus ensuring success. He describes it like this:

> I got better and better at killing. In particular I was so good at the kind of raid I have described that I was taken away from my battalion and set to plan and lead raids further and deeper behind the enemy lines. I came back each time impatient of offers of leave and rest, asking only to be kept active and employed. I volunteered for every difficult and hazardous operation. ... I gave myself no time for anything except war, hoping thereby to escape from my shadows, but they were too adroit for me.[13]

Next, Celliers was sent on a special mission to Palestine. He was stationed at a monastery called Imwash, one of the traditional sites of the ascension of Christ. The monks had vacated the space only days before their arrival, leaving fresh smells of frankincense and myrrh hanging about the cool corridors and gray stone halls.

Almost immediately, Celliers fell ill with malaria. In the past he had recovered quite quickly, but on this occasion the fever wouldn't break. With the help of his batman, Celliers was moved out of the monastery into the open, under the canopy of clouds and stars that he loved so much. There he could be closer to the healing powers of nature.

Being outdoors, as it turned out, only prompted more bouts of delirium. Looking toward the holy shrine that marked the spot where tradition claims that Jesus ascended, Celliers believed he saw Jesus with the disciples. In his hallucination he heard someone say, "Judas is dead! Judas is dead!"

Celliers saw himself, as it were, approaching Jesus and saying, "There are many rumors in Jerusalem and Rome that are not true. See, I am Judas . . . I am alive and I am here."

Celliers believed Jesus took both his hands and helped his fever-riddled body to its feet. Then, looking upward, Jesus exclaimed, "Thank you, Father. Now at last we can both be free."

"But I'm not free," Celliers protested. "I had a brother once and I betrayed him—"

"Go to your brother," Jesus replied, "and make your peace with him even as I have had to do with my need of you."

In that moment the fever broke and sweat poured out like a tropical rain. Celliers determined to visit his brother at any cost, for he would not carry the lie of his betrayal with him to death.

Before breakfast the next day, Celliers summoned a doctor from Jerusalem and secured a month's convalescent leave. Though everyone thought it would be impossible, Celliers then managed to get from Palestine to Egypt and from Egypt to South Africa, with the help of old friends in the South African Air Force.

While driving to his brother's home, Celliers noticed how parched the land was. There was no grass left on the veldt, and the scrub was twisted and burnt black by the sun's fire; sheep and cows were so lean that their ribs and bones seemed about to pierce their taut skins. Vultures circled continually overhead. The smell of death was everywhere.

Failure

Arriving at his brother's home, Celliers approached the front door. Before he could knock, his brother's wife came out. Through a hardened expression she managed to utter a semblance of a greeting. "Well, this is a surprise. Come in and I'll call your brother. He'll be amazed to see you." And then she asked, "Why didn't you send us word you were coming?"

A Christian will find it cheaper to pardon than to resent. Forgiveness saves the expense of anger, the cost of hatred, the waste of spirits.

—HANNAH MORE

"That's a long story," Celliers said, "and I can explain later. But where is he? I'll go and find him."

"Then I'll go on seeing to the dinner," she said. "He's in the garden at the back, giving the last of our water to the trees and vegetables. We've had a terrible time, as you've noticed I expect. No rain for a year. Sheep and cattle dying and all this lovely garden is practically dead." She glanced sharply at Celliers as if he'd been off on vacation rather than fighting a bloody war.

Celliers walked to the back of the house and saw his brother a short distance away, bent over a plant. The blighting hump was even more pronounced in middle age.

In a few strides, they were face to face. In his brother's dark eyes, Celliers saw a life imprisoned from a moment far back in time. "*Ouboet*," he said to his brother, using this Afrikaans term of endearment. "It's good to see you again, *Ouboet*—and still growing things."

The younger brother stammered. "*Ouboet*, um, I wish I'd known, ah, you were coming. I'd have liked to be there to meet you. But come on up to the house. You must be tired. Can you stay long?"

"No," Celliers explained quickly. "In a sense, I've no right to be here at all. It's taken me a fortnight to get here, and I'll be lucky to be back on the front in time if I'm not to get into serious trouble. So I'm going back in a few hours to catch the night train north. I've been hitchhiking my way by air down here. I've come here just to see you."

31

PILGRIM'S PROBLEMS

"Really, *Ouboet*?" he said in disbelief. "Is that really so?"

"I've come all this distance to you because of my great wrong. Of all my failures in life, not one has plagued me more than the time I betrayed you. I am here to ask your forgiveness."

"Oh, but surely, *Ouboet*," he started to protest.

Begging him to listen, Celliers went on to recount in stark detail the events of that late afternoon when he had betrayed his brother. Pained, dark eyes locked with troubled blue eyes and in a broken voice the kid brother managed to say, "You mean you came all the way from Palestine to tell me this? You took the only leave you've ever had from the war to come and tell me this?"

Celliers nodded, too broken up to speak.

"*Ouboet,* you've done many fine things," the younger brother said, "but never a braver one than you've done today. At last we're free of it all, thanks to you." In that moment of love and forgiveness, the brother's love was reborn.

Celliers dismissed himself to prepare for tea. As he reached the steps of the house, he heard a crystal clear tenor voice, silent for decades, beginning to sing:

> Ride, ride through the day,
> Ride through the moonlight
> Ride, ride through the night.
> For far in the distance burns the fire
> For someone who has waited long.

For the first time, Celliers heard a second stanza to the song:

> I rode all through the day,
> I rode through the moonlight
> I rode all through the night.
> To the fire in the distance burning
> And beside the fire found
> He who had waited for so long.

As if by some celestial cue, thunder rumbled deep in the angry sky. The cavalry of the great army of clouds was rounding up the last strays

32

Failure

of blue. The downpour of rain began to revive two shredded, separated lives. Physical rain, yes; but spiritual rain rejuvenated as well. On that day the rain of the Holy Spirit healed the scorched and stricken hearts.

That same Spirit is available to you. He longs to drown your failure today.

BRINGING IT HOME

What mistakes do I most deeply regret? Why?

How can I learn from my failures?

What does the story of Celliers teach me about failure?

Is there anyone with whom God would have me seek reconciliation? Why not do it now?

Write a modern paraphrase of Psalm 51.

Share the story of Celliers with a friend. Discuss specific ways you can practice the lessons from the story.

---

[1] Karen Mains, *With My Whole Heart,* as quoted in *Bible Illustrator,* by Parsons Technology, index 4034.

[2] Psalm 73:26.

[3] Lamentations 3:22, 23.

[4] Laurens van der Post, *The Seed and the Sower* (London: The Hogarth Press, 1963), 48.

[5] Post, 53.

[6] Post, 61.

[7] Post, 76.

[8] Post, 77.

[9] Post, 79.

[10] Post, pp. 87, 88.

[11] Post, 88.

[12] Post, pp. 88, 89.

[13] Post, pp. 117, 118.

CHAPTER TWO

Loneliness

*"Loneliness and the feeling of being uncared for and
unwanted are the greatest poverty."*
—MOTHER TERESA

There's an intriguing line of research on depression that shows one group in our society as being significantly less affected by this mental illness than any other group. Care to guess what the group might be? Left-handers? Blondes? Psychology majors? Boston Red Sox fans? (Fat chance!) What do you think?

To understand the study, first let's take a crash course called Depression 101. While this is a gross simplification of a complex subject, there are two major types of depression. First, there is biologically based depression such as bi-polar disorder, which involves both a manic phase and a depressive phase—real high highs and real low lows. Second, there is psychologically based depression known as reactive disorders. This is triggered more by situations than physiological imbalances.

Disorders like bi-polar depression (that are biologically driven) tend to affect all groups about the same. But reactive depression is more tied to circumstances, like environment, upbringing, and so on. Researchers have identified one group in the United States that experiences significantly less depression of this type than any other. What group?

The Amish. That's right, the buggy-driving folk who have their roots in the early Anabaptist movement in Europe, which took place at the time of the Reformation. The Anabaptists believed that only adults who had confessed their faith should be baptized, and that they should remain separate from the larger society.

Life is full of misery, loneliness, and suffering—and it's all over much too soon.
—WOODY ALLEN

Why does this select group have one-tenth the risk for depression as other Americans? Social scientists point to their strong sense of community. They have effectively found an antidote for loneliness. Perhaps that helps to explain why approximately 90 percent of Amish teenagers choose to stay in their church. (Compare that to Adventist youth who leave the church at an alarming rate of roughly 50 percent.)

Why do so many Amish kids stay committed to their church? The documentary, *Devil's Playground,* offers this explanation by describing the Amish: "It is a tight-knit community, and during the years of running about, it is not surprising that the teenagers eventually seek the comfort, security, and structure of their close-knit community."[1]

Belonging to a church, however, is not an insurance policy against loneliness. Listen to the heart cry of one older woman:

> I sit in the pew next to a warm body every week, but I feel no heat. I'm in the faith, but I draw no active love. I sing the hymns with those next to me, but I hear only my own voice. When the service is finished, I leave as I came in—hungry for someone to touch me, to tell me that I'm a person worth something to somebody. Just a smile would do it, or perhaps some gesture, some sign that I am not a stranger.[2]

Let's face it: We all crave community. We were created in the image of God, who is by nature Three in One—Father, Son, and Spirit. God is the consummate expression of community. Because we possess His nature, we, too, cannot live alone. To live as an island is to seek depression.

PILGRIM'S PROBLEMS

Given our world of highly independent overachievers who try to make it on their own, it's no wonder that one out of six high school students have at least one major bout with depression before graduation. Moreover, 25-30 percent of university students have at least mild symptoms of depression. Although these symptoms may be fueled by more than just loneliness, make no mistake that intimate relationships can counter many of the ailments of depression.

Check out the story in 1 Kings 19. Elijah was so down that he wanted to kill himself. Notice that part of God's therapy for the pouting prophet in the dungeon of depression involved hooking him up with a close friend, Elisha.

The bottom line is this: We were never intended to journey the lowlands of life alone. Erich Fromm had it right when he said, "The deepest need of man is the need to overcome his separateness, to leave the prison of his aloneness."[3]

To some degree, we all suffer through seasons of loneliness. It's estimated that one of every four people reading this book feels lonely. This is especially disconcerting when you consider the most severe form of human torture is not the gas chamber, crucifixion, manual labor, or hanging. The toughest punishment is solitary confinement.

For help in dealing with this problem, consider the words of a very lonely apostle. Paul is staring at the checkered flag in life. The race is almost over. And he is lonely. So in the flickering candlelight of that dank dungeon he pens the immortal words preserved in 2 Timothy 4. Here the apostle identifies the causes and the cures of loneliness.

The causes of loneliness
First, loneliness surfaces in periods of transition. Listen to Paul's reference to the transition before him.

> For I am already being poured out like a drink offering, and the time has come for my departure. I have fought the good fight, I have finished the race, I have kept the faith. Now there is in store for me the crown of righteousness, which the Lord, the righteous judge, will award to me on that day—and not only to me, but also to all who have longed for his appearing.[4]

Loneliness

In a fit of anger a king condemned his most faithful servant to die. Later, the king felt some regret because this servant was the best he had. Softening a bit, the king said to the servant. "I will let you choose how you wish to die."

"Fair enough," the servant smirked, "I choose to die of old age."

I suppose we all want to die of old age. Still, death is an unsavory subject to think about. Even though Paul is an old man and he has lived a full life, there is no easy way to get through this final transition. Paul feels lonely. He is navigating the ultimate transition from life to death. It is during these times of transition that we are particularly vulnerable to loneliness.

When you think about it, our lives are a steady stream of transitions. These transient tendencies are particularly evident in America. During the last five years approximately half of all Americans moved. The average person moves fourteen times over the course of their life. Needless to say, these transitions tear at the fabric of friendships, resulting in a reluctance to develop new and intimate relationships.

Loneliness is the first thing that God's eye nam'd not good.
—JOHN MILTON

Second, loneliness surfaces during periods of separation. Again, listen to Paul's instructions to Timothy: "Do your best to come to me quickly, for Demas, because he loved this world, has deserted me and has gone to Thessalonica. Crescens has gone to Galatia, and Titus to Dalmatia."[5] Demas was a coworker of Paul's who is mentioned in Colossians and Philemon. Some scholars suggest that Crescens was one of the seventy disciples commissioned by Christ. Titus was another close friend to Paul. In fact it is likely that Paul led this Gentile believer to Christ. Paul has been separated from all of his close friends except for Luke, who is mentioned in the next verse. "Only Luke is with me. Get Mark and bring him with you, because he is helpful to me in my ministry."[6] Paul was so lonely he called for the companionship of Mark, who you may recall had deserted Paul in

Pamphylia. When Barnabas wanted to take him on another missionary venture, Paul said, "No, he's already flaked on us once." Paul and Barnabas were deeply divided on this issue of what to do with Mark; consequently, they went separate ways. But now, Paul is so lonely that he even calls for the companionship of Mark.

The soul hardly ever realizes it, but whether he is a believer or not, his loneliness is really a homesickness for God.
—HUBERT VAN ZELLER

Without question, the loneliest season of my life came in the summer of 1982. My girlfriend of seven months, Cherié, (now my wife) and I said goodbye for what we assumed would be forever. She was moving from Washington to Michigan, clearly violating God's will—at least that's what I thought!

Two months elapsed and I couldn't stand it any longer. Everything reminded me of Cherié. I'd drive by McDonald's and think of the time we got ice-cream cones there. I'd smell cigarette smoke and think of the time we went to El Torrito and sat in the nonsmoking section right next to the smoking section. I'd see a person with a nose and think, *Oh, Cherié has a nose too. I've got to see her.* I called constantly but I had to see her.

I couldn't afford to fly to Michigan, so I boarded a bus. For three days and three nights I sat in the belly of a Greyhound.

Upon arrival, I crawled into a refrigerator box that Cherié's mom had wrapped as a birthday present. Cherié ripped into the box. She screamed. I snapped a picture of her tonsils. She then slammed the top back on my head. When she decided it wasn't a dream, she lifted the top once again and smothered my throbbing, bruised head with affection.

If you've ever been separated from people you love, you know it's no fun. In a word, it's lonely.

Third, loneliness surfaces during periods of opposition. Paul had plenty of it. Look at verses 14 and 15: "Alexander the metalworker did me a great deal of harm. The Lord will repay him for what he had done. You too should be on your guard against him, because he strongly opposed our message. At my first defense, no one came to my support, but everyone deserted me. May it not be held against them."[7]

Paul had opposition from Alexander the metalworker. Furthermore, when Paul was put on trial, nobody came to his defense. Everyone opposed him.

Opposition sparks loneliness like nothing else. Some of my lonely moments have coincided with voices of opposition against me. An anonymous letter comes to mind. This person wrote, "Dear Pastor Haffner, I just bought your book *I'd Rather Kiss a Catfish*. At first I thought it was an extraordinary book. I was going to buy 16 copies—one for every one of my grandkids. Then I read page 122…." From there he went into a tirade, berating everything about me because of a nondescript reference to which he took offense. Those kinds of letters often stir feelings of loneliness and a sense that nobody appreciates you.

I do find some comfort, though, in what the world-renowned author and preacher, R. C. Sproul, does when he receives critical letters. In response to his books, he receives many letters that disparage him. He figures that people stay up nights thinking up ways to devastate him. So he asked a friend in public ministry, "Do you ever get any hate mail?"

"I get it all the time," his friend replied.

"Well, how do you handle it?"

"I write them back and say, 'Dear Mr. So and So, I want to warn you about something dreadful. Some lunatic is sending me outrageous letters and signing your name to them.'"

Not a bad way to handle opposition, eh? It's important to do something in order to cope with the loneliness that accompanies opposition.

The cures of loneliness

If your heart is crying out in loneliness, don't despair. There is an avenue of escape. Paul clues us in to the cures for loneliness. How do you cope with loneliness?

The first suggestion that Paul gives us in tackling loneliness is to recognize your needs. Notice Paul's instructions in verse 13: "When you come, bring the cloak that I left with Carpus at Troas, and my scrolls, especially the parchments."[8]

If anyone had a right to participate in a pity party, it would be Paul, right? I'd have pouted, "God, here I've preached my guts out for

You and this is what I get—a damp, rat-infested prison to sit in until they chop my head off."

Paul does not do that. Instead, he was attentive to his physical needs. "Bring my coat," he says. Why? Because he was cold, he was addressing a physical need. No doubt, our loneliness is often exasperated by our own neglect to care for our physical needs. It's easy to numb the pain with junk food and late-night television and overwhelming busyness. All the while the body becomes more and more fatigued. This fuels loneliness.

Notice that Paul does not neglect his mental conditioning either. This prevents him from defaulting into a pity party. He asks for scrolls—that is, papyrus rolls—so that he could read and keep mentally sharp. It's possible that Paul was asking for a file of all his correspondence so that he could defend himself against the reckless charges lodged against him in the Roman court. "But Paul," we might protest, "why do you need scrolls to read? You're going to die any day now." Paul would answer, "I know I'm going to die, but I don't want to die an illiterate dummy. Bring some good books to read."

Paul cares for his spiritual needs as well. He requests the parchments, that is, rolls made of animal skin. Scholars suggest that Paul was asking for his copy of the Septuagint and early copies of the sayings of Christ. His quest for spiritual truth continued until the day he died.

So if you're lonely, take a lesson from Paul and ask yourself some practical questions: Am I caring for my physical needs? Am I eating healthy foods? Am I getting enough sleep? Am I exercising? Am I guarding my thoughts? Am I stimulating my mind with good books that stretch me? Or am I anesthetizing my loneliness by glaring at a television or computer screen all day? Am I spending time in the Word? These physical, mental, and spiritual factors are important in slaying the demon of loneliness.

The second suggestion that Paul offers for tackling loneliness is to minimize your problems. Notice how Paul downplays his problems. "Alexander the metalworker did me a great deal of harm."[9] Notice how Paul does not stew in this injustice. Instead, he leaves retribution in the hands of God. He says, "The Lord will repay him for what he has done.... At my first defense, no one came to my support, but everyone deserted me. May it not be held against them."[10] Notice again how he downplays the fact that his friends abandoned him in his time of need.

To stew in your injustice is to fertilize feelings of loneliness. When you've been done wrong, let it go. Forgetfulness can be a gift from God.

This brings to mind the story of an absent-minded professor who was having breakfast with his family. His wife said to him, "Now, remember. This is the day we move. When you come home, go to the new house and not this one." All day he knew there was something he was supposed to remember, but he couldn't remember what it was. He went home after class, and the house was empty.

We're all sentenced to solitary confinement inside our own skins, for life.
—Tennessee Williams

"Oh yes, we moved. I wonder where we moved to."

He saw some children playing in the yard. He said to a little boy, "Do you know the people who used to live here?"

The boy said, "Yes, sir."

He said, "Do you know where they moved?"

The little boy replied, "Mom said you would forget."

Sometimes—but not always!—forgetting is a good thing. The alternative is remembering. The problem with remembering is that harboring ill-feelings over past injustices is an act of isolating yourself from community. Authentic community flourishes best in an environment of grace. To focus on times when you've been deprived of grace is an act of worshiping your problems rather than connecting with people.

The final suggestion that Paul offers for tackling loneliness is to emphasize God's presence. In his extreme loneliness, Paul could still proclaim, "But the Lord stood at my side and gave me strength."[11]

No matter how lonely you feel, you are never out of God's embrace. John Ortberg uses the metaphor of the cave to describe loneliness. But even in the cave, he argues, God is there. "Finding ultimate refuge in God means you become so immersed in his presence, so convinced of his goodness, so devoted to his lordship that you find even the cave is a perfectly safe place to be because he is there with you."[12]

Ortberg then shares this story:

> A friend of mine, who attended the same graduate school in psychology, wanted to get married. He was quite healthy himself emotionally but seemed to attract dating partners who were lacking. This became discouraging after a while. He was in the dating cave [of loneliness]. When he became a university professor, he used to teach abnormal psychology with a twist: He would illustrate each major category of psychopathology by describing one of his old girlfriends. It was one of the most highly attended classes on campus....
>
> I remember when he finally met the girl who would become his wife—she was a vibrant, devoted Christian and an emotionally healthy person with superb relational skills. She, like him, had a Ph.D. in clinical psychology. My friend finally emerged from the cave. But it was not the last time he would find himself there.
>
> After they were married, the two of them wanted to have children very much. But because she had breast cancer, it looked as though it would not happen. It was cave time again. But then she recovered! Their time in the cave was over. Eventually, they had a beautiful baby girl.
>
> I moved to another part of the country. A few years later they had another child. Then one day I received a phone call. After seven years, the breast cancer had returned. This time it was in her bones and inoperable. And on the answering machine, when she

---

Without friendships
no one would choose to live, even if they
had all other good things in life.
—ARISTOTLE

---

left the message, along with the pain, anxiety and fear, this is what she expressed: "I have never felt God's presence more strongly or have been more sure of God's goodness than I am now."[13]

Loneliness

Like the apostle Paul, she knew that she was about to die. A tidal wave of loneliness engulfed her. But, like the apostle, she could proclaim in absolute certainty: "God is with me. The Lord stands by my side and gives me strength."

Maybe you are in a transition of life and you feel alone. You're about to graduate and you don't know where you're going to live or work. Friend, you are not alone.

Maybe you are separated from your primary community of support and feel isolated. You're parked in the middle of a million people, but you feel desperate because your soul mate is not around. Friend, you are not alone.

You come into the world alone and you go out of the world alone. Yet it seems to me you are more alone while living than even going and coming.

—EMILY CARR

Maybe you are on the receiving end of intense opposition. The evil one is accosting you with doubt and plaguing your life with problems. Maybe you sense an impending divorce or your kids have left the church and they now openly oppose the Christian values you have sacrificed your life to pass along to them, and you feel all alone. Friend you are not alone.

The Lord stands by your side, and He will give you strength. He knows all about loneliness. Picture Him in the moonlit Garden. Clutching the dew-drenched grass, He pours His heart out in anguish. The pressure is so intense that His capillaries crush against His sweat glands, causing His perspiration to glow with a crimson tinge. His blood and tears and sweat glisten in the silver shadows of the Garden.

He staggers to His three closest companions. He has given His whole life for these friends, and where are they now when He really needs them? What are they doing? They snooze away as the Son of God asks them, "Why are you sleeping?"[14] From the Garden Jesus staggers to the Cross.

PILGRIM'S PROBLEMS

The Cross is the ultimate monument of loneliness. It is there that Jesus cries out in anguish, "My God, my God, why have you forsaken me?"[15]

Jesus understands your loneliness. He has been there. So don't despair. As long as He lives, He will make sure that you are never alone.

BRINGING IT HOME

Who do I consider to be my closest friends? Why?

How can God use me to reach out to someone who is lonely?

When was the loneliest time of my life? Why?

How can I be a better friend?

Learn about the Amish at this Web site: <http://www.800padutch.com/amish.shtml>.

Write a psalm entitled "Loneliness."

Keep a list of people whom you suspect are lonely and be a friend to them.

---

[1] Tim Stopper, "Devil's Playground," as quoted at <http://worldfilm.about.com/library/weekly/aafpr042202.htm>.

[2] As quoted by Dr. Edward Watke Jr., "The Problem of Loneliness" at <http://www.watke.org/resources/Problem%20of%20Loneliness.pdf>, 4.

[3] Eric Fromm, *The Art of Loving,* 1956, as quoted from <http://www.quotationspage.com/forum/viewtopic.php?p=3104>.

[4] 2 Timothy 4:6-8.

[5] 2 Timothy 4:9, 10.

[6] 2 Timothy 4:11.

[7] 2 Timothy 4:14, 15.

[8] 2 Timothy 4:13.

[9] 2 Timothy 4:14.

[10] 2 Timothy 4:14, 16.

[11] 2 Timothy 4:17.

[12] John Ortberg, *If You Want to Walk on Water, You've Got to Get out of the Boat* (Grand Rapids, Mich.: Zondervan, 2001), 150.

[13] Ortberg, 150, 151.

[14] Luke 22:46.

[15] Mark 15:34.

CHAPTER THREE

Anger

"What anger wants it buys at the price of soul."
—HERACLITUS

"Sorry, we don't offer an anger management seminar," our office manager, Chris, kindly informed the anonymous caller.

"But I saw it advertised on the reader board at your church," the woman insisted.

"I don't know of anything like that. Perhaps you're thinking of our Lost Relationship Support Group or our Addicts Anonymous."

"Then why are you advertising it on your sign?" the woman snipped.

"I'm in charge of the messages on the reader board, and I know we've never advertised an anger management seminar since I've been here."

"This is North Creek Christian Fellowship of Seventh-day Adventists, isn't it?" The caller's pitch jumped an octave per sentence.

"Yes ma'am, but we don't—"

"There ought to be a law against you *##*#^*#@ Christians who use false advertising to sucker people into your cult."

"I'm afraid you're mistaking us for some other—"

"Why *don't* you offer an anger management class?" the woman demanded. "There's a big need, you know."

Chris couldn't hold her tongue. "Yes, I can see that!" she said, trying to swallow her giggles.

"Noooooo! Dimwit!" the woman exploded. "The class isn't for me! It's for my husband!" Fortunately the woman slammed down the phone before my secretary burst into laughter.

Let's face it: We live in an age of rage. The damage that mismanaged anger does in our society is staggering. The F.B.I. reports that there is one violent crime every twenty-four seconds. There is an aggravated assault every forty-four seconds and a murder every twenty-eight minutes.[1] Among young men, murder is the second leading cause of death; among young women, it's the number one cause of death. Domestic violence continues to scar our homes, and yet little attention is given to the problem.

Approximately 58,000 American lives were lost during the fourteen-year Vietnam War (1961–1975). That is minimal compared to the 491,088 American lives lost over the fourteen years from 1985 to 1998 to gun violence.[2] Since 1980 more men, women, and children have been killed by gunfire in the United States (more than 650,000) than U.S. servicemen and women killed during battle in all of the wars dating from the Revolutionary War to the present.[3] During the Vietnam War, more women were murdered at home than men slain on the battlefield.

> *One of the biggest causes of anger is disappointment over not getting what we expect. We expect life to work out in our favor—we want to be loved and appreciated and all that. But the truth is we'll never get everything we want or expect. If we can accept that fact, it will do a lot to minimize our big disappointments.*
>
> —GARY SMALLEY, *MARRIAGE PARTNERSHIP*, VOL. 14, NO. 1

And it's not just violence. Mismanaged anger plays a major role in virtually every divorce. Even in marriages where there may not be a legal separation, often there is an emotional chasm because of mismanaged anger. Perhaps you've lost a job or a friend due to misguided

Anger

rage. These days, anger is as prevalent as fireworks on the Fourth of July.

Fortunately the Bible is not silent on the subject. Consider this counsel: " 'In your anger do not sin': Do not let the sun go down while you are still angry, and do not give the devil a foothold."[4]

Notice that anger is not forbidden. The biblical counsel is simply that we should express anger in a manner that is not sinful. Furthermore, we're told not to allow our anger to brew overnight.

The wisest man who ever lived offered this advice on anger: "A fool gives full vent to his anger, but a wise man keeps himself under control."[5]

Jesus Himself got angry. "Jesus entered the temple area and drove out all who were buying and selling there. He overturned the tables of the money changers and the benches of those selling doves. 'It is written,' he said to them, ' "My house will be called a house of prayer," but you are making it a "den of robbers." ' The blind and the lame came to him at the temple, and he healed them."[6]

Jesus exploded at the sight of people exploiting the poor. He cleared them out of the temple then remained to heal the blind and the lame. William Barclay comments, "Need is never sent empty away by Jesus Christ. Jesus' anger was never merely negative; it never stopped with the attack on that which was wrong; it always went on to the positive helping of those who were in need. In the truly great man anger and love go hand in hand."[7]

Jesus showed us that anger can be constructive. A modern example of this would be MADD—Mothers Against Drunk Drivers. Like Jesus, the members of that organization leverage their anger toward a positive end.

Scripture clearly teaches the importance of managing anger in a godly way. Although it's important, it's not necessarily modeled well in our world. Instead, we're often tempted to buy into myths that foil our efforts to keep cool. So before we devise a strategy for managing anger, let's dispel some of these myths.

Myths about anger

Myth #1: "My anger is caused by external events and other people."
The *International Herald Tribune* reported the story of a man in

Bellevue, Washington, who became angry when his vehicle got stuck in six inches of snow. He retrieved his tire iron from the trunk and smashed all the windows on his own car. Then he took a pistol and flattened all four tires. Then he reloaded and emptied half of a second clip of bullets into the car. "He killed it," police chief Jack Kellum said. "It's a case of autocide. The man was sober and rational, but very perturbed."[8]

Often we blame inanimate objects for our anger. We also love to blame other people for our anger. You've heard this expressed in quips like, "You make me so mad."

Here's the crucial truth about this myth: In between the event—the stupid inanimate object or the rude person—and the response is my interpretation of the event. Only I can choose my response, be it anger or calm.

Who, then, really makes you mad? You do.

Only you can take responsibility for the management of your anger. This is an important distinction to make, especially in a world that shuns personal responsibility for acts of mishandled anger.

Take, for example, the issue of road rage. Not surprisingly, most drivers blame the "other guy" for the increase in aggressive driving and road rage. In a USA Today/CNN/Gallup Poll, 74 percent of respondents said others are driving more aggressively than five years ago, but only 13 percent said they drive more aggressively than five years ago. Almost half, however, admitted to an act of road rage in the past five years.[9]

An incident in Dallas, Texas comes to mind. In February 1997, a delivery van driven by a thirty-three-year-old man collided with a pickup truck driven by a forty-two-year-old man. A side mirror was broken in the minor collision.

The delivery driver got out of the van and argued with the pickup driver. The delivery man started punching the older man as he sat in his truck. The pickup driver pulled out his licensed, concealed, .40-caliber handgun and shot the assailant in the chest.

Police charged the shooter with murder, but a grand jury refused to indict him. He was cleared in the incident. After all, it was the other man who had caused the incident. The murderer was provoked. He couldn't help himself.[10]

Anger

Give me a break! Let's not be fuzzy on this one. Do not play the game of rationalizing your mismanaged anger because of what someone else has done. Don't minimize the damage it can do. Remember, only you can make you mad.

Myth #2: "I can't control my anger."

Bunk. You can control your anger if the stakes are high enough.

One time Cherié and I were having a doozie of an argument. Consumed in rage, I slammed our cordless telephone on the floor. It bounced, and at the pinnacle of its ascent, it rang.

Picture it. I am screaming, "Well if you're so perfect then why don't you—"

Riiiinnnng.

Then in the sappiest pastoral drool I could muster, I abruptly stopped and answered, "Hello, *Pastor* Haffner speaking."

Suddenly I had full control over my temper. Amazing how fast we can change, isn't it? The point is, you—and only you—*can* control your anger.

Myth #3: "The best way to handle your anger is to let it rip."

There is a theory in anger management that suggests the best way to deal with anger is to explode and get it off your chest. The theory is that if you do not vent your anger, it will build and build within you like steam in a teakettle. Fail to provide release and you'll blow up like a volcano.

> *Anybody can become angry—that is easy;*
> *but to be angry with the right person,*
> *and to the right degree, and at*
> *the right time, and for the right purpose,*
> *and in the right way—that is not within*
> *everybody's power and is not easy.*
> —ARISTOTLE

Pastor John Ortberg exposes the flaws inherent in this theory by suggesting that this logic would be ludicrous if applied to any other emotion. For example, he points out that you never hear somebody say, "I've been holding in joy all these years. People have been telling funny jokes and I've been repressing my laughter and I haven't released it. Joy has been building up inside of me and now the joy dam is about to burst and I'm going to spew joy all over everybody."

Therapists never say, "Listen, friend, you better get in touch with your gratitude, because when you were growing up people did a lot of things for you and you never verbalized your thankfulness. Now you got all this gratitude bottled up inside of you and it's not healthy. You're like a walking time bomb of happiness. Someday it's going to go off and you're going to go up to people you don't even know and just spew gratitude all over them, 'Thank you, thank you, thank you.' "[11]

---

*D*oomed are the hotheads!
Unhappy are they who lose their cool and
are too proud to say, "I'm sorry."
—ROBERT HAROLD SCHULLER

The erroneous assumption of this theory is that people defuse once they've exploded. In fact, the opposite is true. When people hit or shout, they feel powerful, and naturally they want to hit or shout more. It becomes a sadistic circle.

Managing your anger

Rather than making excuses for our anger, doesn't it make more sense to manage it? After all, anger will be a constant companion through life. The children's story called *Touching Spirit Bear* reminds us of this fact. The tale tells of a wise Indian mentor who grabs a stick to provide an impromptu lesson about anger. The wise man calls the left end of the stick "anger" and the right end "happiness." Next, the teacher instructs the student to break off the left end of the stick to get rid of his anger. Try as he might, however, the student could never make the left end disappear. The lesson? You can't get rid of all anger. That isn't even the goal. The goal is to manage anger wisely and well. How? Here's a four-step strategy.

Anger

Step 1: Freeze!

When you're angry, take a lesson from technology; always count down before blasting off. Before you react, freeze. Recite the words of Solomon: "A quick-tempered man does foolish things, and a crafty man is hated."[12]

This first step is perhaps the most difficult because anger is, by definition, physiological arousal. As the arousal increases, people suffer from what some psychologists call "cognitive incapacitation." Simply put, they can't think straight.

Ralph Milton knows about cognitive incapacitation. He sheepishly remembers the morning he was awakened at 5:00 A.M. by a loud pounding on his roof. Still in his pajamas, Ralph went into the backyard to investigate. He found a woodpecker on the TV antenna, "pounding its little brains out on the metal pole." Angry that the little creature had ruined his sleep, Ralph picked up a rock and threw it. The rock sailed over the house, shattering the windshield of his car. In utter disgust, Ralph took a vicious kick at a rock fence, only to remember—too late—that his freshly broken foot was unprotected by a shoe. Uncontrolled anger, as Ralph learned, can result in foolish actions. Robert Ingersoll put it this way: "Anger blows out the lamp of the mind."[13]

A football player from the University of Kansas could testify of the truth in this proverb. This 6'3" 270-pound tackle got so incensed at Taco Bell when they shorted him a chalupa that he got out of his car and attempted to crawl through the 14"-by-46" drive-through window. To no one's surprise, he got stuck. The frightened manager and employees locked themselves in an office and called the police. When the police arrived, they laughed hysterically as they watched the legs and back end of the football player kicking in midair. Police sergeant George Wheeler said, "When you take a big guy and put him through a small space, something's got to give."[14]

Take this verse to the bank: "A quick-tempered man does foolish things."

Step 2: Think!

Champions at anger management live by this text: "A wise man thinks ahead; a fool doesn't and even brags about it!"[15] So next time someone steams your beans, you're going to freeze and buy some time. With that time you're going to think about the most mature way to deal with the situation.

Someone recently sent me a story via email that illustrates what this looks like. Seems a man and woman had been married for more than sixty years. They shared everything. They had talked about everything. They held no secrets from each other, except for one. The woman kept a shoebox in the top of her closet that she warned her husband never to open. In all their years of marriage, he rarely thought about the box. But one day, the little old woman got very sick, and the doctor said she would not recover. In trying to sort out their affairs, the old man retrieved that shoebox at his wife's request. The time had come to disclose the contents of the box.

Speak when you are angry and you will make the best speech you will ever regret.
—AMBROSE GWINNETT BIERCE

He lifted the lid to discover two crocheted doilies and a stack of money totaling over $25,000. He asked for an explanation.

"When we were engaged," she said, "my grandmother told me the secret of a happy marriage was to stop and think before blowing up when I got angry. She told me that if I ever got mad at you, I should just keep quiet and crochet a doily before saying anything."

The little old man was so moved he had to fight back tears. Only two precious doilies were in the box. Apparently she had only been angry with him twice in all their years together. "Honey," he beamed, "that explains the doilies, but where did all this money come from?"

"Oh," she said, "that's the money I made from selling the doilies."

Next time you feel angry, crochet a doily. Use the time to think through the consequences of your response.

Step 3: Listen!

The next step involves cleaning out your ears. James, the half-brother of Jesus, offers this counsel for managing your anger: "My dear brothers, take note of this: Everyone should be quick to listen, slow to speak and slow to become angry, for man's anger does not bring about the righteous life that God desires."[16]

Anger

This statement has very important insight. Notice the three elements: listening, speaking, and getting angry. Generally, the angrier you are, the more you want to talk and the less you care to listen. Here's the way it works according to the Bible: If you are quick to listen and slow to speak, you will be slow to anger. The reverse is also true. If you are quick to jump in, and you're not in the listening mood, you'll be quick to get angry. So you must cultivate the habit of listening.

Have you ever had a conversation with somebody who doesn't listen and loves to finish your sentences? One time George Will was in a debate with William F. Buckley, Jr. and Buckley kept cutting him off. Finally George Will quipped, "Mr. Buckley, I am the world's foremost expert at how I want to finish my sentences."

The Bible teaches that "even a fool is thought wise if he keeps silent, and discerning if he holds his tongue."[17] When you're angry, before you respond, listen. Try to hear with your heart.

Recently Cherié and I took our two girls to get our picture taken for a new church directory. We arrived at the fellowship hall only to see a long backup of people snaking out the door. But they insisted, "You go ahead, Pastor. You've got a one-year-old and a six-year-old who probably don't care to wait. Go on, it'll just take a minute, right?"

"Oh, sure. Sure!"

Decked out in their charming, matching dresses, the girls followed us into the makeshift studio. We figured the photo would double as a Christmas card. We were just one quick click away from capturing a picture of the happy Haffner clan.

Right.

It's not that our kids were wild. They didn't throw tantrums, and they weren't defiant; they were just scared—particularly Claire, our youngest. Some strange guy with some weird apparatus was trying to make them smile, holding up odd shapes that frightened them. So they cried.

To reply to a nasty remark with another nasty remark is like trying to remove dirt with mud.

—ANONYMOUS

PILGRIM'S PROBLEMS

But we wanted a happy picture. Because if you send people a Christmas card with two bawling kids, it's not a good thing (not to mention having this picture in the church directory).

We tried and tried until everybody in the church was waiting and watching in line. We had no option but to give up.

"Well," we reasoned, "no doubt it was because we went in the evening when the kids were tired. Let's try again in the morning." So a couple days later we went to Sears for another photo op.

At Sears, we waited for twenty minutes because there was another girl, the same age and size as Claire, who was in the modeling zone. The photographer couldn't stop snapping. She'd say, "Sweetie, cock your head an inch to the left" and this one-year-old would dutifully obey. She smiled perfectly, never fussed. I was really happy for the parents. They'd have a cute Christmas card.

As soon as we entered the studio, the nightmare flared all over again. We didn't get one decent shot. So we rescheduled.

Our final pass at this found Daddy and Mommy gently negotiating, as if talking with terrorists. "Tell you what," I bargained. "You girls smile for one picture and we'll take our happy family to a happy place like TCBY right after the happy photo. OK?"

The wrath of God is as pure as the holiness of God. When God is angry he is perfectly angry. When he is displeased there is every reason he should be. We tend to think of anger as sin; but sometimes it is sinful not to be angry. It is unthinkable that God would not be purely and perfectly angry with sin.
—STUART BRISCOE

Sure, they were into that—until we entered the studio. Once again, the cameras triggered the tears. So my tune changed. "Either stop your crying," I steamed, "or I'll *really* give you something to cry about."

What would make a grown man resort to this? I can't tell you.

Anger

Finally Lindsey suggested, "Daddy, can we just prop up my doll in Claire's chair instead of Claire?"

It was tempting.

But now, imagine the scene assuming that I had tuned in to Claire's little heart. Suppose I listened to her, not hearing her screams with just with my ears, but hearing her heart—plugging into what she was really trying to tell me.

Had I listened, I would have seen the ordeal through the eyes of a one-year-old: bright lights, bossy strangers, stressed parents—no wonder she was scared. Had I listened, it would have informed my response and pacified my anger.

So listen carefully. Then move on to the final step.

Step 4: Act!

Everything to this point is immaterial unless we take the final step and act appropriately. Listen to Jesus describe this final step of action.

"But I tell you that anyone who is angry with his brother will be subject to judgment."[18] There are two Greek words for anger. One is the type that explodes quickly but dissipates immediately. The other is the type that lingers and broods for a long time. The word in Matthew 5:22 describes the long-lasting anger.

Jesus goes on: "Again, anyone who says to his brother, '*Raca,*' is answerable to the Sanhedrin. But anyone who says, 'You fool!' will be in danger of the fire of hell."[19]

Jesus reserved some of His harshest words for those who misman-age anger. Then He says something that, in His day, was so radical that it would have probably set off some murmuring in the crowd. Listen to Jesus' next statement: "If you are offering your gift at the altar and there remember that your brother has something against you, leave your gift there in front of the altar. First go and be reconciled to your brother; then come and offer your gift."[20]

To appreciate the revolutionary nature of this statement, you have to understand the strict protocol that surrounded temple behavior in ancient days. In no way was it acceptable to just leave the temple while making a sacrifice.

Even in our day we have generally accepted rules of etiquette for church. These rules are mostly unwritten, but we all know them. For example, you should show up on time; don't talk when the organist is playing; turn off your cell phone; don't snore; don't bring a TV; don't leave early, and so on. This is common courtesy stuff in church.

Now take the generally accepted rules of etiquette for church in our day and multiply them many times over, and you get a sense of the obsession that church leaders had in Jesus' day for acceptable behavior in the temple. You didn't go to the synagogue late. You didn't disturb people sitting around you in the synagogue. And you never left early— ever! The rules were rigid.

In the middle of such rigidity, Jesus said there is one circumstance where you should shatter the generally accepted church etiquette and just leave. The circumstance? When there is unresolved anger. If there is anger between you and a sister or brother, you must act. It's that important.

Maybe you need to take this final step. You have resentment that has been boiling for weeks or months toward a family member or a colleague, and it's destroying you. So will you have the courage to act? Jesus would say to you, "Get out of church and address the unresolved anger with your brother or sister. You can't truly worship until you have taken this final step of action." Ignore the counsel of Christ on this one, and your soul is at peril. As the Chinese proverb puts it, "So long as a man is angry he cannot be in the right."

Father expected a good deal of God. He didn't actually accuse God of inefficiency, but when he prayed, his tone was loud and angry, like that of a dissatisfied guest in a carelessly managed hotel.
—CLARENCE SHEPARD DAY, JR.

You really can manage your anger wisely and well. Remember the acronym FTLA—freeze, think, listen, act.

So what does the theory look like with skin on it? I think of a close friend whom I would have never guessed had a problem with anger. He's a mild-mannered pastor. But like all pilgrims, he struggles

Anger

to honor God in his anger. Here's the story in his words:

> The problem was a classmate who ridiculed and verbally tormented everyone in his path. In my anger, I had gone to my father for advice. "There may come a time when you just have to 'pop' 'em," he said. I didn't expect those words from my father. In fact, nothing was more foreign to his nature.
>
> Sure enough, the day arrived. I had absorbed a belly-full of abuse when his attention shifted to a girl sitting behind me. It was time. With all the force a fifth-grader could muster, I swung for his belly. Yes, the punch had anger behind it, but it came from a strange mixture of humiliation, chivalry and fear. I was fortunate that he found it incredibly funny, or I might have wound up with a black eye.
>
> Since then, communication became my approach to handling anger. Then I had children.
>
> The loud bang brought my wife running. Her nine-month-old son was screaming, but safe and unharmed in his crib. I, her husband, was sitting in the corner fighting tears. Brandon had been crying for two hours. I was trying to be a good dad and let Mom get some rest, but nothing seemed to work. In frustration, desperation and filled with the desire to "pop 'em," I had smashed my fist into the closet door. Now, with a sore hand and a hurting heart, I realized how close I had been to hitting my own child. I was horrified at my humanity.
>
> Anger control isn't my problem. But I know, my wife knows, and God knows, that it can be. Now, when I begin to feel anger building toward my wife or my children, I step into another room and say a prayer of thanks and pleading. "Thanks" that God has blessed me with a very special family and "pleading" that He will fill me with godly wisdom and love.
>
> I want to be the kind of Father He is to me.[21]

BRINGING IT HOME

When's the last time I felt really angry? Did I handle the situation in a Christlike way? If not, what will I do differently next time?

PILGRIM'S PROBLEMS

What myth about anger am I most inclined to believe? Why?

Have I ever suffered from "cognitive incapacitation" because of my anger? If so, when?

Is God calling me from the altar in order to address any unresolved conflicts in my life?

Do a word search in the Bible and read every reference to anger.

Scan a newspaper and note any stories that are rooted in mismanaged anger. Check out this Web site: <http://www.angermgmt.com>.

---

[1] As quoted from <http://www.gabrielalarms.com/statistics.htm>.

[2] As quoted from <http://www.newmoononline.com/ggg/facts.htm>. Source: Centers for Disease Control, National Vital Statistics Reports, Vol. 48, No. 11, July 24, 2000.

[3] As quoted from <http://www.newmoononline.com/ggg/facts.htm>. Source: WAVE (Wisconsin Anti-Violence Effort) Educational Fund, 1999/2000.

[4] Ephesians 4:26, 27.

[5] Proverbs 29:11.

[6] Matthew 21:12-14.

[7] William Barclay, *The Gospel of Matthew, vol. 2* (Edinburgh, Scotland: Saint Andrew Press, 1975), 248.

[8] *International Herald Tribune,* 19 January 1982, as quoted from <http://www.fpcbellevue.org/sermons/html/2002-11-03.htm>.

[9] Jeff Langley, "Steer clear of speeding moron motorists," 1997, as quoted from <http://www.texasonline.net/langley/columns/rage.htm>.

[10] Ibid.

[11] John Ortberg, "All About Anger, Anger Myths" (M9607) (South Barrington, Ill.: Seeds Tape Ministry, a ministry of Willow Creek Community Church, 1996).

[12] Proverbs 14:17.

[13] As quoted at <http://humanityquest.com/topic/Quotations/Index.asp?theme1=anger>.

[14] Wayne Rice, ed., *Hot Illustrations for Youth Talks 4* (Grand Rapids, Mich.: Zondervan, 2001), 187.

[15] Proverbs 13:16, TLB.

[16] James 1:19, 20.

[17] Proverbs 17:28.

[18] Matthew 5:22.

[19] Ibid.

[20] Matthew 5:23, 24.

[21] Written by Monte Torkelsen. Used by permission.

CHAPTER FOUR

Loss

*"No matter how hard the loss, defeat might serve as
well as victory to shape the soul and let the glory out."*
—AL GORE, SR.

Some years ago I heard Dr. Gerald Sittser share a heart-wrenching lecture on loss. He is a professor of religion at Whitworth College in Spokane, Washington. His story is that of losing three generations of his family in an instant.

In the fall of 1991, his wife of nineteen years, Lynda, was home schooling their two oldest children. To teach the chapter on Native American culture she arranged to visit an Indian reservation in rural Idaho. On the appointed Friday afternoon, the family, including all four kids along with Gerald's mother, went to the reservation for a powwow. There they had an opportunity to talk with tribal leaders about problems Native American Indians face in the modern age. Ironically, as it turned out, the leaders spoke primarily of the abuse of alcohol.

After the powwow, the Sittsers piled into their minivan, buckled up, and headed for home. By then it was dark. Ten minutes later, Dr. Sittser noticed an oncoming car flying down on a lonely stretch of highway. He slowed down at a curve but the other car did not. It jumped its lane and smashed head-on into their vehicle. The driver was Native American, drunk, and driving eighty-five miles per hour. He was accompanied by his pregnant wife, also drunk, who was killed in the accident.

Let's pick up the story now as Dr. Sittser shares it in his powerful book, *A Grace Disguised*:

PILGRIM'S PROBLEMS

I remember those first moments after the accident as if everything was happening in slow motion. They are frozen into my memory with terrible vividness. After recovering my breath, I turned around to survey the damage. The scene was chaotic. I remember the look of terror on the faces of my children and the feeling of horror that swept over me when I saw the unconscious and broken bodies of Lynda, my four-year-old daughter Diana Jane, and my mother. I remember getting Catherine (then eight), David (seven) and John (two) out of the van through my door, the only one that would open. I remember taking pulses, doing mouth-to-mouth resuscitation, trying to save the dying and calm the living. ...

In one moment my family as I had known and cherished it was obliterated. The woman to whom I had been married for two decades was dead; my beloved Diana Jane, our third born, was dead; my mother, who had given birth to me and raised me, was dead. Three generations—gone in an instant!

That initial deluge of loss slowly gave way over the next months to the steady seepage of pain that comes when grief, like floodwaters refusing to subside, finds every crack and crevice of the human spirit to enter and erode. I thought that I was going to lose my mind. I was overwhelmed with depression. The foundation of my life was caving in.

...I was lifted momentarily out of space and time as I knew it and was suspended somehow between two worlds.

One was the world of my past, so wonderful to me, which was now lying in a tangle of metal on the side of the road; the other was the world of my future, which awaited me at the end of that long ride to the hospital as a vast and frightening unknown. ...By some strange twist of fate or mysterious manifestation of divine providence I had been suddenly thrust into circumstances I had not chosen and could never have imagined. I had become the victim of a terrible tragedy.[1]

Dr. Sittser's story brings to mind the Bible story of Rizpah, an obscure tale that also offers valuable lessons on loss. Rizpah was one of King Saul's lovers who bore him two sons, Armoni and Mephibosheth.

Loss

Although she moved in the elite circles of the imperial palace, Rizpah suffered loneliness and poverty. She was one of thousands of victims of the turmoil in her day.

I will welcome happiness, for it enlarges my heart; yet I will endure sadness, for it opens my soul. I will acknowledge rewards, for they are my due; yet I will welcome obstacles, for they are my challenge.
—Og Mandino

Rizpah was a victim of spiritual turmoil. She lived during a time of moral rebellion. Idol worship was rampant. Sexual immorality was as common as casinos in Vegas. The Israelites had abandoned Yahweh.

Rizpah was also a victim of political turmoil. She was trapped in the holocaust of wars and political coups. The political unrest dated back to the time when Saul broke an oath that Joshua had made with the Gibeonites. The promise not to destroy the Gibeonites had been sealed in Yahweh's name. But when Saul came to power he scoffed at the covenant. This brash and arrogant king didn't care about promises Joshua had made. *He* was king. *He* would determine what covenants were worth keeping. Consequently, the political backlash for Saul's arrogance bit innocent victims like Rizpah.

Rizpah was also a victim of economic turmoil. A severe famine devastated the land of Israel for three years. Children with watermelon bellies and barely enough skin to stretch over their ribs lined the streets of Jerusalem. Scripture informs us that the famine was the consequence of Saul's slaughter of the oath-protected Gibeonites. Against this backdrop of spiritual, political, and economic unrest, Rizpah struggled to survive. Then tragedy struck.

To get revenge on the Israelites for breaking the oath, the Gibeonites demanded that seven of Saul's sons be hanged in payment. Innocent children had to die for the sin of their father.

On that fateful day, the Gibeonites marched Rizpah's two sons up the hill. A burly Gibeonite bullied her boys, wrapping a noose around each child's neck. In one jerking motion, he snuffed out their lives. Rizpah screamed in horror. There was nothing she could do. She was a victim. Her loss stands as a monument to the senselessness of human suffering.

> *All thought worth thinking is conceived in the furnace of suffering.*
> —THOMAS CARLYLE

Our next glimpse of Rizpah offers a sharp contrast to the savage slayings, for this heartbroken mom could not leave her sons. Although her boys were dead, Rizpah stayed with them—fighting off the vultures and hyenas. Picture the ghastly scene: seven bruised bodies hang from trees while Mom shoos away the beasts that are keen to gorge on the kill. For six months, Rizpah protects the decaying bones of her boys. Although she had no power to prevent the gruesome murder of her sons, she could engage in the loving act of mercy by caring for their bodies on the gallows tree. Day after weary day, Rizpah watched. The foul stench of the rotting corpses soured the air. The gory video of her boys' last breaths replayed in her mind. Finally, at the end of the barley harvest, Rizpah buried the skeletons.

When King David heard Rizpah's story, he was touched by this mother's love. He remembered that the bones of Saul and Jonathan were still in the streets of Beth-shan. So he commanded that the bones be recovered and mingled with the precious bones which Rizpah had guarded. Together they were to be buried in the family grave at Zelah.

Lest you think I'm fabricating the story, read it for yourself from Scripture:

> But the king took Armoni and Mephibosheth, the two sons of Aiah's daughter Rizpah, whom she had borne to Saul, together with the five sons of Saul's daughter Merab, whom she had borne to Adriel son of Barzillai the Meholathite. He handed them over to the Gibeonites, who killed and exposed them on a hill before the LORD. All seven of them fell together; they were put to death during the first days of the harvest, just as the barley harvest was beginning.

Loss

Rizpah daughter of Aiah took sackcloth and spread it out for herself on a rock. From the beginning of the harvest till the rain poured down from the heavens on the bodies, she did not let the birds of the air touch them by day or the wild animals by night. When David was told what Aiah's daughter Rizpah, Saul's concubine, had done, he went and took the bones of Saul and his son Jonathan from the citizens of Jabesh Gilead. (They had taken them secretly from the public square at Beth Shan, where the Philistines had hung them after they struck Saul down on Gilboa.) David brought the bones of Saul and his son Jonathan from there, and the bones of those who had been killed and exposed were gathered up.

They buried the bones of Saul and his son Jonathan in the tomb of Saul's father Kish, at Zela in Benjamin, and did everything the king commanded. After that, God answered prayer in behalf of the land.[2]

It is a dramatic story indeed—as is Gerald Sittser's story. Often, sensational stories such as these grab the headlines and seem to dwarf the losses that are not so extreme, and so we often quantify loss and compare by asking, "Whose loss is worse?" But it's worth noting here that loss is loss, whatever the circumstances. All losses are bad, only bad in different ways. Each loss deals a unique pain.

> *I can look back at my darkest periods and realize that these were the times when the Lord was holding me closest. But I couldn't see his face because my face was in his breast—crying.*
>
> —JOHN MICHAEL TALBOT

Consider the story that Dr. Sittser mentions of Leanna, a mom who was diagnosed with multiple myeloma—an incurable form of cancer. Her loss is slow but sure. The landscape of her life is decaying slowly, one square inch at a time. Her pain persists. She worries about her two teenage children and her husband, who has Parkinson's disease. So whose loss is worse? Rizpah's? Sittser's? Leanna's?

I think of a friend who is suffering intense loss through a divorce. He is plagued by bitter memories and regrets of how his relationship could have been different. Who's to say his loss is not as painful as one like Gerald Sittser's?

What about parents who battle infertility? Some friends of mine were once informed of a baby that would be available for adoption. Their hopes soared. The would-be parents filled out piles of paperwork and waited anxiously for the birth. They decorated the baby room. They stuffed the closet with new clothes. But on the day of birth, the mom opted to keep the child. Six years later now, the room still sits decorated but unused. Is their pain any less?

In the end I agree with Dr. Sittser, who writes:

> Everywhere there is pain, human misery, and tragedy. ...
>
> Whose loss is worse? The question begs the point. Each experience of loss is unique, each painful in its own way, each as bad as everyone else's but also different. No one will ever know the pain I have experienced because it is my own, just as I will never know the pain you may have experienced. What good is quantifying loss? What good is comparing? The right question to ask is not "Whose is worse?" It is to ask, "What meaning can be gained from suffering, and how can we grow through suffering?"[3]

Let's explore the answers to that question. Since we are all victims of loss at various junctures in life, let's learn how we can live beyond the loss. I offer three suggestions.

Confront the corpse

One thing that Rizpah gets right is that she courageously enters into her tunnel of pain. She camps out at the site of horrific anguish, and she stays there until healing begins.

Gerald Sittser tells about a recurring nightmare in which he was chasing the setting sun. He was frantically running west, trying desperately to catch it and remain in its fiery warmth and light. But of course he always lost the race. The sun always beat him to the horizon and was soon gone. He'd fall, exhausted, looking behind him to the east at the foreboding darkness about to bury him. He wanted to keep chasing the sunset, but he knew it was futile.

Then his sister gave him this advice: The quickest way for anyone to reach the sun and the light of day is not to run west, chasing after the setting sun, but to head east, plunging into darkness until one comes to the sunrise. Sittser writes:

> I decided from that point on to walk into the darkness rather than try to outrun it, to let my experience of loss take me on a journey wherever it would lead, and to allow myself to be transformed by my suffering rather than to think I could somehow avoid it. I chose to turn toward the pain, however falteringly, and to yield to the loss, though I had no idea at the time what that would mean.[4]

A natural reaction to pain is to escape via avenues of avoidance. By seeking to avoid the corpse at all costs, we cope with the pain. What are these coping mechanisms?

> *Man can endure almost any suffering if he can see a purpose or meaning in it. Conversely, he will be miserable even amidst great luxury if he cannot relate his life to some larger context which makes it meaningful.*
> —Viktor Frankl

For example, one avenue would be denial. Some years ago I visited friends at the hospital to congratulate them on the birth of their first child. What was supposed to be a merry celebration, however, proved to be misery. After the delivery, the doctor informed the parents that their child had Down syndrome. With no advance warning, the news hit them like a wrecking ball to the heart. The mother's reaction was to deny it. For days she refused to touch or hold or look at her child. Instead she demanded the baby be kept out of the room while she engaged in trivial small talk with relatives about the weather, the Red Sox, and the latest episode of *Friends*.

---

*O*ur lives have become so antiseptic that we honestly believe we've suffered adversity and experienced affliction if our Reebok shoes pinch our toes, if our car is in the shop and we must take the bus, or if we find a bug in our water glass. Meanwhile, much of the world's population can't afford shoes, travel only where they can get by foot, and often die for lack of food and water.

—S. RICKLY CHRISTIAN

"Isn't she beautiful? Look at her precious little ears," a family member cooed, trying to encourage the mom. But there was no reply. She felt that she had to deny reality.

This is not an unusual reaction to loss. People in denial often refuse to accept loss for what it is, something terrible that cannot be reversed.

A second popular coping mechanism is to indulge carnal appetites. I remember my deep disappointment the first time Cherié lost a child through a miscarriage. At night I found it difficult to sleep, so instead I would retreat to my office and numb my mind with computer games. Then I'd plant myself in front of the TV and watch infomercials. It wasn't that I was in the market for the latest, greatest ab-exerciser, but rather, I didn't want to face reality. Many grieving people hold suffering at bay by working sixty hours a week, eating too much, or indulging sexual fantasies or some other carnal appetite in order to steer clear of the corpse.

We naturally resist confronting the corpse and entering into the night of reality. Maybe you do not want to face the truth: The relationship is over, and there is nothing you can do to bring reconciliation. The rape really happened, and the searing memory will remain a constant companion. The friend died, and there's nothing you can do to bring him back. Whatever your story, healing begins by confronting the corpse.

Loss

Control what you can

There is a second principle of living beyond loss that emerges from Rizpah's story. Rizpah had no control over the political or economic or spiritual upheaval of her day. She had no control over her sons' deaths. She was a victim of hostile and brutal circumstances. But she would not surrender to passivity. She would defend her boys even after their tragic deaths by confronting the hyenas at night and the vultures by day. While there were many things that Rizpah could not control, that which she could control she did so with undaunted courage and unrelenting pertinacity. Once again, listen to Dr. Sittser:

> There is little we can do to protect ourselves from [losses]. They are as inevitable as old age, wrinkled skin, aching bones, and fading memory. There is much we can do, however, to determine how to respond to them. We do not always have the freedom to choose the roles we must play in life, but we can choose how we are going to play the roles we have been given.
>
> Choice is therefore the key. We can run from the darkness, or we can enter into the darkness and face the pain of loss. We can indulge ourselves in self-pity, or we can empathize with others and embrace their pain as our own. We can run away from sorrow and drown it in addictions, or we can learn to live with sorrow. We can nurse wounds of having been cheated in life, or we can be grateful and joyful, even though there seems to be little reason for it. We can return evil for evil, or

---

The only cure for suffering is to face it head on, grasp it round the neck, and use it.
—MARY CRAIG

---

we can overcome evil with good. It is this power to choose that adds dignity to our humanity and gives us the ability to transcend our circumstances, thus releasing us from living as mere victims.[5]

PILGRIM'S PROBLEMS

A lot of things in life we cannot control, but there is one thing we can always control and that is our ability to choose how we will respond.

In 1995, Cherié and I endured a season of sorrow that felt as if it would destroy us. In the course of two months, I accepted a call to pastor a new parish, which meant job transitions for Cherié and me. It was tough because we left a church that we had founded and loved for seven years. At the same time Cherié gave birth to our first child. We were staying temporarily with Cherié's parents because of their invaluable support through all the changes. Suddenly Cherié's mom died of a heart attack.

> *I* will not die an unlived life. I will not live in fear of falling or catching fire. I choose to inhabit my days, to allow my living to open me, to make me less afraid, more accessible, to loosen my heart until it becomes a wing, a torch, a promise. I choose to risk my significance; to live so that which comes to me as seed goes to the next as blossom and that which comes to me as blossom, goes on as fruit.
>
> —Dawna Markova

Next we moved into an apartment complex that was infested with mice. The apartment was so bad that one time I left a bag with a couple of packs of gum on the bed and an hour later returned to discover the mice had devoured nearly every stick of gum. Apparently four out of five dentists make chewing recommendations to rodents as well as human beings. Needless to say, it was not a good place to care for a newborn.

In the midst of this upheaval, I was working on an assignment for *Insight* magazine about Viktor Frankl, the Holocaust survivor. Frankl's brother, wife, and parents died in the camps. Frankl wondered if his path would lead to the gas ovens or if he would be among the lucky ones to shovel the victims.

One day, alone and naked in a cell, he discovered what he later called "the last of human freedoms"—the freedom his Nazi captors could never strip from him. They could rape him of every convenience. They could torture him to death. But they could never touch one thing—his freedom to choose how he would respond. Listen to what Frankl writes:

> The experiences of camp life show that man does have a choice of action. There were enough examples, often of a heroic nature, which proved that apathy could be overcome, irritability suppressed. Man can preserve a vestige of spiritual freedom, of independence of mind, even in such terrible conditions of psychic and physical distress.[6]

As I sat in my mouse-infested apartment writing that article, it occurred to me, Frankl is right. There were a lot of things I could not control—traumatic loss, the hardship of transition, and so on. But I could control how to respond.

Celebrate still

I love the way Rizpah's story ends. "They buried the bones . . . and did everything the king commanded. After that, God answered prayer in behalf of the land."[7] Even a story as horrific as Rizpah's offers hope and cause for celebration. God sent the rain and brought healing to His people.

Scholars point out an intriguing parallel between Rizpah and Mary, the mother of Jesus. Both watched as their son was hanged. In Rizpah's story we have a shadow of Golgotha. Seven innocent men were hanged, or as the Latin version put it, crucified, to make atonement for the Israelites' sin against the Gibeonites. In Mary's story, Christ was hanged to make atonement for us all. Because Christ was hanged, however, we can be restored to the Father. Even in a story so tragic we can find hope and healing.

Dr. Sittser found cause to celebrate in his story as well. He writes, "Loss requires that we live in a *delicate tension*. We must mourn, but we must also go on living. We might feel the world has stopped, though it never does. Grass keeps growing, bills continue to mount, houses get dirty, children need raising, jobs must be done, people must be cared for. . . ."[8]

Sittser concludes with this thought:

> I will never recover from my loss and I will never get over missing the ones I lost. But I still cherish life—Monica and Todd,

my children and the privilege of raising them, deep friendships, service to college and community, moments of worship and quiet reflection, good books to read, summer hobbies. Moreover, I will always want the ones I lost back again. I long for them with all my soul. But I still celebrate the life I have found because they are gone. I have lost, but I have also gained. I lost the world I loved, but I gained a deeper awareness of grace. That grace has enabled me to clarify my purpose in life and rediscover the wonder of the present moment.[9]

I don't envy those who have never known any pain, physical or spiritual, because I strongly suspect that the capacity for pain and the capacity for joy are equal. Only those who have suffered great pain are able to know equally great joy.
—MADELEINE L'ENGLE

In spite of what happens we must still celebrate the good. A story by Rudy Giuliani illustrates this. The former mayor of New York City tells of attending a funeral the week before September 11, 2001. The service was a tribute to a young firefighter, Michael Gorumba, who died while battling a blaze on Staten Island. At the funeral, Giuliani met the young man's mother, Mrs. Gorumba. He learned that over the past ten months Mrs. Gorumba had also lost her father and her husband—both suddenly.

Ironically, the wedding of Mrs. Gorumba's daughter was planned for the following month. Relatives urged Mrs. Gorumba to postpone it, but she would hear nothing of it. Giuliani writes:

> I was amazed. Here was a woman in the throes of the worst tragedy possible—the loss of a child—yet she was speaking calmly, drawing her words from a reservoir of courage that was unimaginable to me. Later, I asked, "How do you deal with such a horrible loss?"
>
> Mrs. Gorumba looked at me. "When terrible things happen,"

she said, "I try to concentrate on the good parts of life and celebrate them even more than I had before. Think about it. At this
very moment I have two things in front of me: dealing with my
son's death—which I have to do and will do—and dealing with
my daughter's wedding. I choose to focus on the wedding. Why?
Because life is a combination of great tragedy and great beauty.
This family will deal with our tragedy. But we will also celebrate
the beauty of this wedding with even greater joy. This is what my
son would want, and this is what my daughter needs."[10]

The next day, Mrs. Gorumba, accompanied by her daughter, approached Giuliani with this request: "Could you walk my daughter
down the aisle? After all, this girl has lost all the male relatives in her
life, and there's no one left to give her away on her wedding day."

"I would be honored," Giuliani replied.

Shortly after the request, terrorists toppled the twin towers and
Giuliani's world became insanely frantic. He tells of racing from Tuesday
to Saturday and not being able to remember ever eating or sleeping.

On Saturday, the day before the wedding, reporters asked him:
"Will you still attend the wedding?"

"Absolutely," he replied.

And so it was that the mayor of New York City escorted Mrs.
Gorumba's daughter down the aisle—something he had never done
before because his only daughter was twelve years old at the time.
Giuliani writes:

> I remember feeling that this moment was not only impor-
> tant for the bride and her family, but for the community as
> well. And, frankly, it was especially wonderful for me. In the
> space of a week, I had seen the worst that life can offer, this
> grim national calamity, but with God's good grace, I then lived
> to see the best part of life, a beautiful young couple so much in
> love, looking forward to a life together.
>
> Mrs. Gorumba was right—it was something to celebrate.[11]

I remember Giuliani's story whenever life vomits its worst on me.
For even in the darkest of nights there are still sunbeams of joy.

PILGRIM'S PROBLEMS

Whatever the losses and tragedies of your life, there is still something to celebrate. You can flourish even through misfortune. You can live above loss. How? Confront the corpse, control what you can, and celebrate still.

BRINGING IT HOME

In what ways have I been a victim?

How would I feel if I had no freedom of choice?

Are there any corpses in my life that I am afraid to confront? If so, what are they?

How do I choose to respond when I am a victim?

How can I honor God through seasons of loss?

How can I most effectively minister to people going through hardship?

Write a commentary on Isaiah 53. Read it whenever you feel overwhelmed by sorrow.

Discuss this question with friends: Why is there suffering in the world?

Write a list of one hundred reasons you have to celebrate.

---

[1] Gerald Sittser, *A Grace Disguised* (Grand Rapids, Mich. Zondervan, 1995), ch. 17–21.

[2] 2 Samuel 21:8-14.

[3] Sittser, 29, 30.

[4] Sittser, 34.

[5] Sittser, 37, 38.

[6] Viktor Frankl, *Man's Search for Meaning* (New York: Washington Square Press, 1984), 86.

[7] 2 Samuel 21:14.

[8] Sittser, 41.

[9] Sittser, 68.

[10] Rudolph Giuliani, *The Right Words at the Right Time,* ed. Marlo Thomas (New York: Atria Books, 2002), 119.

[11] Giuliani, 123.

CHAPTER FIVE

Resentment

"Resentment builds up slowly and quietly in the rear recesses of our souls. After awhile it becomes almost comfortable...like a shield protecting us from the light of truth. It's a little like an old shoe that's comfortable, casual, cherished...and smelly."
—DERRIC JOHNSON

When I first read the story, it seemed too far-fetched to be real. So I called an optometrist and asked, "Could this be true?" While he said it would be extremely rare, he figured it could happen.

Here's the story: A little boy named Julian stumbled while chasing butterflies in a field of tall grass. Soon afterward, the boy's left eye started hurting. His doctor couldn't find the source of irritation, so he prescribed some ointment and sent him home.

It seemed the problem was solved. About a year later the boy complained of cloudy vision. His parents took him to an eye specialist who was stunned by what he discovered.

Apparently when Julian had fallen a year earlier, a tiny grass seed was implanted in his cornea. Slowly the seed had grown and had begun to sprout microscopic leaves in Julian's eye. The seed had to be removed immediately in order to save the boy's vision.[1]

Can you believe it? A seed is such a small thing. But left untended, in the wrong place for a long enough period of time, it can do enormous damage.

The same principle rings true with issues of the soul. I'm not talking about grass seed, of course; rather, small seeds of resentment that left unchecked can sprout in the soul and cause untold damage.

Perhaps you have seeds of resentment in your spirit:

PILGRIM'S PROBLEMS

An angry parent who intimidated you into silence planted a seed that still grows.

A classmate swiped your hard work and scored a higher grade than you.

Holding on to anger, resentment and hurt only gives you tense muscles, a headache and a sore jaw from clenching your teeth. Forgiveness gives you back the laughter and the lightness in your life.

—JOAN LUNDEN

A parent abandoned you.

A date that started innocently enough ended in rape.

An ex-spouse wiped out your bank account and also won custody of the kids.

A trusted elder in the church betrayed you.

A mother-in-law continually reminds you that you will never quite measure up.

A pastor failed to visit you during a season of sorrow.

An unfaithful spouse finds happiness after the divorce.

An employer forced you into early retirement and now you face feelings of futility and loneliness.

No doubt we could go on and describe a field packed with seeds of resentment. Once again this is a problem most pilgrims face. Ignore it and it's like a Chia Pet that keeps growing and wrecks your heart. So let's look to see what Scripture can teach us on the topic.

I suppose that if any Bible character had the right to resentment it would be Joseph, don't you think? How tempting it must have been for him to live in a chronic state of resentment against his dad, his brothers, his boss's wife, his boss, and God. Yet somehow Joseph uprooted the weed that threatened to destroy him and he triumphed over resentment.

Remember the story? Pastor John Ortberg describes it as a classic good news/bad news tale.

Resentment

Joseph is his daddy's favorite: That's very good.

But his brothers hate his guts: That's very bad.

His daddy gives him a beautiful coat: That's very good.

But his brothers rip it off, cover it with blood, pretend he's dead, sell him into slavery in a distant land: That's very bad.

He lands a job in Egypt's Silicon Valley working for Potiphar—a wealthy, not-too-bright boss with a laissez-faire management style. Potiphar likes him, so Joseph is extremely empowered. He's promoted to work in the front office and ends up in charge of everything—he is on the cover of *Forbes* and *Business Week*. Plus, he's a strikingly handsome man, sort of like Tom Cruise, but taller and better-looking. This is all very good.

Potiphar's wife thinks he's good-looking and tries to seduce him. This is very bad.

Joseph resists. Very good.

But the wife is furious. She lies to her husband and gets Joseph arrested. Since Egypt does not have good sexual harassment legislation on the papyrus at this time, Joseph is shafted. Very bad.

In prison Joseph meets Pharaoh's butler, interprets a dream that predicts the butler will get paroled, and arranges for the butler to get Joseph's release. Very, very good.

But the butler forgets, and Joseph languishes in prison. Very, very bad.[2]

---

*A*nger will never disappear so long as thoughts of resentment are cherished in the mind. Anger will disappear just as soon as thoughts of resentment are forgotten.

—JOHN DRYDEN

The story seesaws back and forth from good news to bad news. But through the roller coaster, Joseph never succumbs to resentment. How tempting it must have been to resent his dad for showing him preferential treatment. Or to resent his brothers who betrayed him

75

and sold him to Midianite merchants. Or to resent Potiphar's wife for framing him. Or to resent Potiphar for unjustly sending him to jail. Or to resent the cupbearer for forgetting about him. Or to resent God— after all, Joseph modeled stellar integrity and faithfulness, and look where it got him. How is it possible to go through an ordeal like Joseph's and not be strangled by the sprouting seeds of resentment?

Consider three passages in the story that provide insight in dealing with resentment.

First, remember that God is with you
The text reminds us twice that God was with Joseph.

> Joseph's master took him and put him in prison, the place where the king's prisoners were confined. But while Joseph was there in the prison, the LORD was with him; he showed him kindness and granted him favor in the eyes of the prison warden. So the warden put Joseph in charge of all those held in the prison, and he was made responsible for all that was done there. The warden paid no attention to anything under Joseph's care, because the LORD was with Joseph and gave him success in whatever he did.[3]

In the last chapter we grappled with Dr. Gerald Sittser's tragic loss. Here now is the rest of his story.

The case went to court. Sittser's attorney assured him that this case was a slam-dunk. Surely the drunk driver would be incarcerated for a long time. When the case came to trial, however, the drunk driver was released on a technicality. This man's heinous crime—the murder of his own wife and child in addition to three generations of the Sittser family—went unrequited.

You can only imagine the overwhelming sense of resentment that Dr. Sittser felt. Listen to how he describes it:

> During the months that followed the trial I thought often about the driver of the other car. I fantasized reading reports in the newspaper that he had died hideously or that he had committed a crime that put him behind bars for life. I wanted

to see him suffer and pay for the wrong I believed he had done. I even dreamed of being in another accident with him. His car collided with mine. It was clearly his fault, as I believed it was the first time. But on this occasion a crowd of hundreds witnessed the accident and volunteered to testify against him.

It eventually occurred to me that this preoccupation was poisoning me. It signaled that I wanted more than justice. I wanted *revenge*. I was beginning to harbor hatred in my heart. I was edging toward becoming an unforgiving person and using what appeared to be the failure of the judicial system to justify my unforgiveness. I wanted to punish the wrongdoer and get even. The very thought of forgiveness seemed abhorrent to me. I realized at that moment that I had to forgive. If not, I would be consumed by my own unforgiveness.[4]

If broken relationships are tolerated, the body cannot build itself up in love. The power of a church will be found in the capacity generated by healthy relationships. Resentment is such a dangerous thing. It's like drinking poison and waiting for the other person to die. If there is resentment in the body, the grace of God is truncated.
—WAYNE CORDEIRO

Through this whole agonizing ordeal, like Joseph, Sittser kept running into reminders of God's presence. The Lord was with him. Listen to how Sittser concludes that chapter:

As I look back now, I see that no matter where I turned after my loss, I kept running into God. I shivered before the randomness of my suffering. I asked, "Why me?" I wrestled with unforgiveness. The questions I asked, the temptations I faced, the revenge I sought, the bewilderment I felt, and the grief I experienced all pushed me inexorably toward God.[5]

How was it that Joseph could be the victim of such extreme injustice and still triumph over resentment? It was because Joseph lived in the presence of God. When you feel the seeds of resentment growing in your spirit, run into the presence of God. Living in the presence of Jesus is like dousing weeds of resentment with an ocean of Roundup.

Second, remember that God will soften the sting

Notice where this counsel emerges in Joseph's story. "Before the years of famine came, two sons were born to Joseph...Joseph named his firstborn Manasseh and said, 'It is because God has made me forget all my trouble and all my father's household.' "[6]

As was customary in ancient times, Joseph chooses a name for his oldest son that held deep significance. The Hebrew word for Manasseh means "to forget." This is not to suggest that he had no memory of how he had been wronged. The name Manasseh can be literally translated, "God has taken the sting out of my memories."

You've heard the phrase "forgive and forget." Well, it's impossible to forget the tragic injustice of a loved one's death. Make no mistake, forgiving someone doesn't mean that you condone them or their actions. It doesn't mean that you excuse what they did. It doesn't mean that you have no recollection of being wronged. It doesn't even mean that you have reconciled with them. Forgiveness is the act of letting go of your right to hurt back someone who has hurt you. Forgiveness means giving up the right to get even.

Our fatigue is often caused not by work, but by worry, frustration and resentment.
—DALE CARNEGIE

Amy Tan, the author of best-selling novels such as *The Joy Luck Club*, provides a wonderful picture of this. She refers to her feeling of resentment as "a storm in my chest," which she battled because she grew up in a very dysfunctional home. She recounts an incident when she was sixteen. Like a fury of hailstones, her storm exploded in statements directed at her mother. "I hate you. I wish I were dead."

Resentment

In response, her mother stood upright, "her lips stretched in a crazy smile. 'Okay, maybe I die too,' she said between huffs. 'Then I no longer be your mother.'"[7] Amy admits her mother had plenty of storms in her chest, too. At times she threatened to kill herself by dashing into the street, holding a knife to her throat.

I think a compliment ought to always precede a complaint, where one is possible, because it softens resentment and ensures for the complaint a courteous and gentle reception.

—MARK TWAIN

For days after such blowups, Amy's mother would not talk to her. She tormented her, constantly criticized her, and seemed to seize every opportunity to humiliate her. Amy swore to herself that she would never forget the injustices. She would never relinquish her resentment. Amy later said, "I resolved to store the injustices, harden my heart, and make myself as impenetrable as she was."[8]

Many years later when Amy was forty-six, she was working on a novel about a girl and a mother when the phone rang. Surprisingly, it was her mother. For the past three years, her mother had been losing her mind to Alzheimer's. It started with little things like forgetting to lock her door, but soon declined to the place where she couldn't identify any of her friends or family.

Listen now as Amy tells her story:

"Amy-ah," [my mom] said, and she began to speak quickly in Chinese. "Something is wrong with my mind. I think I'm going crazy."

I caught my breath. Usually she could barely speak more than two words at a time in years. "Don't worry," I started to say.

"It's true," she went on. "I feel like I can't remember many things. I can't remember what I did yesterday. I can't remember what happened a long time ago, what I did to you . . ." She spoke as a person might if she were drowning and had bobbed to the surface with the force of will to live, only to see how far she had already drifted, how impossibly far she was from the shore.

She spoke frantically. "I know I did something to hurt you."

"You didn't," I said, "really, don't worry."

"I did terrible things. But now I can't remember what…and I just want to tell you…I hope you can forget just as I've forgotten."

I tried to laugh so she would not notice the cracks in my voice. "Really, don't worry."

"Okay, I just wanted you to know."

After we hung up, I cried, both happy and sad. I was again the same sixteen-year-old, but the storm in my chest was gone.

My mother died six months later. By then she had bequeathed me her most healing words, those that are as open and eternal as a clear blue sky. Together we knew in our hearts what we should remember, what we can forget.[9]

Amy Tan had a Manasseh experience. She found the freedom in forgetting. It's not that she couldn't remember the painful shadows of her childhood; rather, the sting was softened. She found healing from her resentment.

You can too. God can soften the sting.

Finally, remember that God's justice will prevail

In this promise of justice, we are granted the freedom to let God be God. Again this notion comes out of Joseph's story. After Jacob dies, Joseph's brothers fear that Joseph's resentment will surface. The biblical account reads like this: "His brothers then came and threw themselves down before him. 'We are your slaves,' they said.

"But Joseph said to them, 'Don't be afraid. Am I in the place of God? You intended to harm me.' "[10] Notice, Joseph still holds them accountable—he does not ignore the horrific injustice that his brothers caused. But then he replies, " 'You intended to harm me, but God intended it for good to accomplish what is now being done, the saving of many lives. So then, don't be afraid. I will provide for you and your children.' And he reassured them and spoke kindly to them."[11]

Resentment

Even though the brothers intended great harm, God took the injustice and used it to accomplish His purpose. In the end, we really can trust God, but we must allow God to be God.

As a cognitive decision, forgiveness frees people to separate their thoughts of resentment and bitterness from their feelings of hurt, thus bringing their negative thoughts under the fruit of the Spirit of self-control.
—FREDERICK DIBLASIO

Once again, listen to Gerald Sittser's observations:

> However difficult, forgiveness in the end brings freedom to the one who gives it. Forgiving people let God run the universe. They let God punish wrongdoers as he wills, and they let God show mercy as he wills too. That is what Job and Joseph came to....That is also what Jesus decided, as demonstrated by the pardon he granted his accusers and executioners while dying on the cross.
>
> ...Ultimately every human being will have to stand before God, and God will judge every person with wisdom and impartiality. Human systems may fail; God's justice does not.[12]

Coming to this conclusion was most helpful in my own battle against resentment. As a child I endured a painful episode of mistreatment. For decades my parents wondered how their boy changed so dramatically, almost overnight. They told me later, "We couldn't understand how suddenly you turned into this angry, uncontrollable little monster." I vaguely remember visiting psychiatrists in my parents' quest to discover answers. They wondered for decades. Little did they or I know that seeds of resentment were planted. For years these seeds grew uncontested in my heart.

PILGRIM'S PROBLEMS

It wasn't until I was in college that I stared down the ugly fruit of resentment. That's when I received the news that this man who I so deeply resented (although I had no clue how much I resented him) had died.

My initial reaction scared me, shocked me, and shamed me. I'm sorry to admit that my first thought was, *Good! I hope it was a slow, lingering, painful death.* It was my first clue that unveiled how much resentment had accumulated in my heart through the years. I felt guilty harboring such thoughts.

> *A*ny work done faithfully and well is difficult. It is no harder for me to do my job than for any other person, and no less. There are no easy tasks in the Christian way; there are only tasks which can be done faithfully or erratically, with joy or resentment.
> —EUGENE PETERSON

It was a professor in the psychology department who helped me see that my resentment would destroy me. He was a very wise man who helped me see that it is not my duty to enact justice. Nor is it within my power to right the wrongs against me. In the end, I really can trust God to be God. His justice will prevail and I don't need to obsess over evening up the score.

Now I'm wondering about you. Are there seeds of resentment growing in you? Left unchecked, they will wreck your heart. Resentment will destroy your soul. Resentment will suck the joy out of your life. So remember, even through the evil injustice of this world, God is with you. Your calling is to live in the presence of Jesus. That's the first and most important thing. As you live in the presence of Christ, He will soften the sting of the sins committed against you. And make no mistake, in the end His justice will prevail. Someday all things will be made new and we will live in a place of perfect grace and justice. You've got His Word on it.

Resentment

BRINGING IT HOME

Do I have any seeds of resentment growing in me? If so, what are they?

In what ways can an unforgiving spirit damage me?

What does it mean for me to live in the presence of Jesus today?

What stings do I need for God to soften?

How can knowing that God's justice will prevail help me to cope with the pain of injustice?

Write a personal definition of resentment.

Journal any feelings of resentment that come to mind. Burn the paper as a tangible symbol of releasing these feelings to God.

Read Gerald Sittser's book, A Grace Disguised.

---

[1] Wayne Rice, ed., *Hot Illustrations for Youth Talks 4* (Grand Rapids, Mich.: Zondervan, 2001), 81.

[2] John Ortberg, *If You Want to Walk on Water, You've Got to Get out of the Boat* (Grand Rapids, Mich.: Zondervan, 2001), 98.

[3] Genesis 39:20-23.

[4] Gerald Sittser, *A Grace Disguised* (Grand Rapids, Mich.: Zondervan, 1995), 119, 120.

[5] Sittser, 132.

[6] Genesis 41:50, 51.

[7] Amy Tan in Marlo Thomas, ed. *The Right Words at the Right Time* (New York: Atria Books, 2002), 339.

[8] Tan, 339.

[9] Tan, 340, 341.

[10] Genesis 50:18, 19

[11] Genesis 50:19-21

[12] Sittser, 127.

CHAPTER SIX

Guilt

*"The purpose of being guilty is to bring us to Jesus.
Once we are there, then its purpose is finished. If we
continue to make ourselves guilty—to blame
ourselves—then that is sin in itself."*
—CORRIE TEN BOOM

On a recent trip to Washington, D.C., I was waiting to speak at an employee appreciation banquet. Spotting an empty chair, I asked the man next to it, "Do you mind if I join you?"

"No, not at all. Have a seat. I'm Jack. I think you know my wife, Bonnie."

"Really, how so?"

When he told me her maiden name I remembered her well. Moments later, she joined us and it all came rushing back.

After exchanging the expected pleasantries, she confessed, "I still feel guilty whenever I think of you. Do you remember the time you and Tom asked Lucy and me to the banquet?"

Remember? How could I ever forget? It's not that we just "asked" them to a banquet—we beseeched them. We wooed them. We labored for seven hours meticulously crafting an invitation engraved in calligraphy. We even hired a man dressed as a thirteenth-century scribe to deliver the scroll to these "two fine damsels of Hadley Hall."

We waited for their reply. And waited. And waited. Only after every student on campus had plans for *the* social extravaganza of the year did the girls get back with us. Their reply came by way of a piece of lined notebook paper with a message scribbled in pencil:

Guilt

Dear Karl and Tom,

Sorry it took us so long to reply. Sam and Jeff asked us to the banquet too, so we're going with them. Sorry! Thanks for asking.

Your friends,

Bonnie and Lucy

You can understand why I grimaced a bit when Bonnie queried, "Do you remember . . .?"

Nonchalantly, I replied, "Um, ah, let's see, yeah, I do *vaguely* remember that."

Later, my wife, Cherié, joined us at the table. When Bonnie introduced herself, Cherié squealed, "Ooooh! *You're* the Bonnie with Lucy that burned Karl and Tom—"

"Yes! I'm *that* Bonnie! I told Karl I still feel a little guilty over that."

Guilt is an interesting thing, isn't it? I marvel that twenty-three years later a chance meeting between former classmates could trigger a twinge of guilt. Truly, sometimes it lingers in the heart for decades. In Bonnie's case it launched belly laughs over a trivial matter. But others are gobbled up by guilt—and it's no laughing matter.

A line from *Moby Dick* comes to mind: "Miserable man! Oh! most contemptible and worthy of all scorn; with slouched hat and guilty eye, skulking from his God; prowling among the shipping like a vile burglar hastening to cross the seas."[1] Ever feel like that?

---

*C*ruel with guilt, and daring with despair, the midnight murderer bursts the faithless bar; invades the sacred hour of silent rest and leaves, unseen, a dagger in your breast.

—SAMUEL JOHNSON

The famed psychiatrist Dr. Karl Menninger once said that if he "could relieve the patients in psychiatric hospitals of their guilt and convince them that their sins were forgiven, seventy-five percent of them could walk out the next day."[2] Truly, guilt is wrecking a lot of lives. But before you give in to guilt, it's important to understand that there are two types: good guilt and bad guilt.

Shame and guilt are noble emotions essential in the maintenance of civilized society, and vital for the development of some of the most refined and elegant qualities of human potential.
—WILLIARD GAYLEN

First, the good guilt: This guilt is God's way of initiating dialogue that leads us to healing. Listen to the prophet Isaiah: " 'Let's talk this over!' says the Lord; 'no matter how deep the stain of your sins, I can take it out and make you as clean as freshly fallen snow.' "[3] Good guilt is the vehicle through which we feel as clean as freshly fallen snow.

Recently I was cruising in my '87 Corolla when the oil light flashed on. I immediately stopped and checked the oil. It was bone dry. Fortunately the oil light alerted me that something important needed my attention. Had I ignored the light, I would have wrecked the engine.

Good guilt works like that. It serves as the warning light of the conscience. Pay attention to it. It can prompt you to take preventive action that will safeguard your heart.

Think about tragic times in history when good guilt has been ignored. Take, for example, Hermann Göering, the designer of some of the worst evil in Nazi Germany during WWII. Eventually he came to trial at Nuremburg for his hideous deeds of hate. While the attorney was reading a horrifying list of crimes, Hermann Göering leaned over to another man on trial, Albert Spear, and said, "Never mind. Someday they'll build monuments to us."

Here is a person partly responsible for the death of millions and millions of human beings, and yet he mused of memorials that would be made for him! For Göering, a glimpse of guilt might have sparked a sliver of humanity in his stony heart.

Guilt

But there is also bad guilt. This can languish for decades. It produces feelings of worthlessness and hopelessness. David wrestled against this overwhelming burden of bad guilt. Listen to the way he describes it:

> My bones are brittle as dry sticks because of my sin. I'm swamped by my bad behavior, collapsed under gunnysacks of guilt. The cuts in my flesh stink and grow maggots because I've lived so badly. And now I'm flat on my face feeling sorry for myself morning to night. All my insides are on fire, my body is a wreck. I'm on my last legs; I've had it—my life is a vomit of groans.[4]

Can you sense David's burden of bad guilt? He likens it to maggots in the soul.

I once made an impromptu comment in a sermon that was interpreted by some as a disparaging remark against the local police department. While I did not mean it in that way—I have great respect for these men and women who serve our community with distinction and excellence—it was still a thoughtless comment that offended some of the officers. All afternoon I berated myself for saying such a stupid thing. Finally that night I attempted to make amends. I called all of the officers that I could reach and apologized. Each officer was very gracious and accepted my apology.

Psychiatrists require many sessions to relieve a patient of guilt feelings which have made him sick in body and mind; Jesus' power of spiritual and moral persuasion was so overwhelming that he could produce the same effect just by saying: Thy sins be forgiven thee.
—MALCOLM MUGGERIDGE

That night—even though I had done everything I could to take care of the situation—a nagging voice still seared my conscience. I had a nightmare. Normally I can't remember my dreams, but this one was different. I dreamed that the next morning, I was rolling out of my driveway attempting to fasten my seatbelt and the back wheels of my car reached the street just a second before I clicked the buckle. But because I had driven an inch on public roads without a seatbelt, the police arrested me. Policemen jumped from every rooftop and tree in the neighborhood. Their machine guns were pointed at my head as they screamed, "Freeze, Mr. Haffner—you're under arrest for driving without a seatbelt. You're going to jail! Ha, ha, ha, ha, ha!"

That's bad guilt. That guilt keeps you awake at night after you've done everything in your power to repair the wrongs.

An itinerary for your guilt trip

Since guilt can be good or bad, how is it possible to leverage guilt in a constructive way? Because guilt can be an ally, canceling the guilt trip may not be wise; but how then do you make the most of the guilt trip? Consider this simple itinerary:

First, sum it up. Start by taking inventory of the causes for your guilt. Determine if your guilt is valid. If it is, deal with it. If it isn't, discard it.

Take, for example, Mr. Barwick. He had a circulation problem in his leg but refused to allow the recommended amputation. As the pain became unbearable, though, he finally consented to the surgeon's advice.

Before the operation he asked the doctor, "What do you do with legs after they are removed?"

"We do a biopsy, then we incinerate them," the doctor replied. "Why do you ask?"

Mr. Barwick made a bizarre request. "I would like you to preserve my leg in a pickling jar. I will put it on my mantle. Then I can taunt it and get even for the pain it has caused me." He got his wish. But the despised leg had the last laugh.

Mr. Barwick suffered from the condition known as phantom limb. Locked somewhere in the brain of some amputees is the memory of the nonexistent hand or leg. Invisible toes curl, imaginary hands grasp things, an amputated leg feels sturdy enough to stand on. Despite the fact that the amputated leg rested on his mantle, Mr. Barwick could still feel the torturous pressure of the swelling as the muscles cramped.

So it is with false guilt. The taunting pain whispers of shame that is nonexistent. False guilt is common: guilt about the parents' divorce, guilt over abuse in childhood, guilt about failure to live up to child-hood dreams. False guilt clings like a sticky spider's web doused in superglue. So start by summing up the reason for guilt. If it's true guilt, address it. If it's false guilt, discard it.

Fess up. The second stop on our itinerary is to confess. If it's valid guilt, then admit it. David once said of himself, "I recognize my faults. I'm conscious of my sin."[5] On another occasion, he declared, "I decided to confess them to You and You forgave all my sins."[6] Confess your sin.

---

*R*eligion *without guilt just tries to make God a big "pal" of man.*
—A. W. TOZER

The word for confession in the Bible is *homologeo, homo* meaning "same," *logeo* meaning "speak." *Homologeo* means to speak the same. It means to agree with God and pray, "God, You're right. We're of the same mind on this one. I blew it. I sinned. I failed."

Look up. The next step then is to look to God as the source of forgiveness for sin. The Bible puts it this way: "Let us draw near to God with a sincere heart in full assurance of faith, having our hearts sprinkled to cleanse us from a guilty conscience and having our bodies washed with pure water."[7] Herein is the key to dealing with guilt: "Let us draw near to God." It always circles back to this invitation to live in the presence of Jesus. For that is where we find strength. You can't get rid of guilt using your own strength any more than you can live a victorious Christian life in your own power. Frederick Buechner once said this:

> It is about as hard to absolve yourself of your own guilt as it is to sit in your own lap. Wrongdoing sparks guilt sparks wrong-doing *ad nauseam*, and we all try to disguise the grim process from both ourselves and everybody else. In order to break the circuit we need somebody before whom we can put aside the disguise, trusting that when he sees us for what we fully are, he won't run away screaming with, if nothing worse, laughter.[8]

PILGRIM'S PROBLEMS

Only in Jesus do we find this kind of pardon from guilt.

A product called "Disposable Guilt Bags" once appeared in the marketplace. It consisted of a set of ten ordinary brown bags with the following instructions: "Place the bag securely over your mouth, take a deep breath and blow all your guilt out, then dispose of the bag immediately." Believe it or not, the Associated Press reported that 2,500 kits were quickly sold at $2.50 per kit![9]

Wouldn't it be nice to dispose of guilt so readily? However, it's not that easy. You cannot fix yourself. What makes it possible to be forgiven, to be cleansed, to receive our life back again, is the cross of Jesus Christ. So look up and find freedom from guilt in God alone.

Give it up. The final stop in this guilt trip itinerary is to surrender. Isaiah once wrote, "The Lord says, 'Do not cling to the events of the past or dwell on what happened long ago. Watch for the new thing I'm going to do.' "[10]

William Wordsworth said it three hundred years ago: "From the body of one guilty deed a thousand ghostly fears and haunting thoughts proceed."[11] It's true. Uncontested guilt will hurt your heart.

Maybe you know that all too well. Perhaps you opted for an abortion and the guilt still plagues you. Maybe you embezzled a lot of money and you can't afford to make it right. Maybe you recently put an aging parent in a nursing home against her will and guilt is a constant companion.

Whatever it is, please know that there is freedom from guilt. Forgiveness flows freely from the Cross. Of course, you may need to reconcile with people you have wounded. And the consequences may linger. But still, you can find freedom from guilt.

Guilt

One more trip

We started with a trip to D.C. Then we tackled the guilt trip. Now let's take one more trip—this time to Boise, Idaho.

I did everything to avoid this woman on the plane. She had been sitting directly in front of me, but when a gentleman asked if he could take her seat to sit with his boy, she was happy to accommodate. She plopped herself in the center seat of our row. Jumping up, I searched for another. No such luck. I reluctantly resigned myself to my original row.

My seat assignment did provide the opportunity to practice my spiritual gift—eavesdropping. I listened closely as the man on the other side of this elderly woman explained, "I have been gone for seven days, and I miss my wife so much. We've been married for twenty-two years, but we've never been apart this long before."

Since I was going to a wedding, I hoped to pick up a sermon illustration from this man. I leaned over, straining to hear him. That's when my elbow slipped off the armrest and landed in the lady's lap.

With a face that looked like Santa's suit, I stammered to explain my invasive behavior. "I'm sorry," I said, "but I was trying to hear his story since I'm flying to Boise to officiate at a wedding."

The woman's eyes swelled to the size of kiwis. "You're a pastor?"

"Yes."

"Let me just apologize to you right now. I feel guilty whenever I'm around pastors!"

Then she told me why. "The most hateful, hurtful words that I have ever spoken, I said to a pastor. You see, many years ago when my husband was beating me black and blue and bloody, I confided in my pastor, who strongly advised me to get a divorce. Well, I've never believed in divorce. I didn't like his suggestion, so I uncorked on him. I told him if he didn't believe in the sanctity of marriage then I had no respect for him.

"The pastor countered, 'But you don't have a marriage.'

"My husband's behavior only got worse. And to think, my husband did all this while he was a colporteur."

"Colporteur?" I interrupted. That word sounded strangely Adventist to me. So I asked her, "You wouldn't be a Seventh-day Adventist, would you?"

"Why yes! Are you one as well?"

"Indeed."

PILGRIM'S PROBLEMS

Guilt is perhaps the most painful companion of death.

—ELISABETH KÜBLER-ROSS

She went on to share how she left the church. "But, oh, how I missed it. For seven years I was homeless—living out of my '69 pickup. No matter what town I was in, however, I always looked up the local Adventist church in the Yellow Pages and then I'd sit in my truck and watch the people file into church while I sat and bawled. I so desperately wanted to join them, but I felt too guilty. I finally returned to church. The people were very gracious that first Sabbath back. I've been attending ever since."

I asked her about the pastor who advised her to leave her husband. Ironically, he is a friend of mine.

"You don't say?" The woman was stunned. After a long pause she asked, "Would you deliver a note to him?"

"I'd be happy to."

She started to write, but was so anxious that her hand was trembling like a paint-can shaker. So she talked while I wrote. Here's the letter I delivered the next week:

> Dear Pastor,
> I have always loved you, and I ask for your forgiveness because I wasn't a nice person when you suggested there is no marriage to save—you were right. I was re-baptized in 1994. All those years I was out, but now I'm back. I ask forgiveness and praise God He's allowed me back into the church in spite of myself. Although I tried to run from God, He was always in my thoughts. For that, I'm very grateful.
> Sincerely, Georgine[12]
> P.S. I'm still married to the same old boy, but I haven't seen him since 1983.

When we landed in Boise, Georgine hugged me goodbye. "I feel like God orchestrated this divine appointment."

"No doubt in my mind," I agreed.

Guilt

Retrieving her luggage from the carousel, she said, "I'm getting my bags, but the heaviest bags—the suitcases of guilt that I've carried all these years—I'm letting God take care of them for me. Thank you for delivering my letter to the pastor."

BRINGING IT HOME

Why is it difficult to forgive myself?

On a scale of one to ten, how guilty do I feel right now? Why?

If I could redo one mistake of my past, what would it be and why?

What counsel would I give to somebody who struggles with nonproductive guilt?

Learn a new hymn that addresses the topic of guilt.

Think about someone who may harbor feelings of guilt against you. Do what you can to bring healing.

Ask a mature follower of Christ for his/her perspectives on guilt.

[1] As quoted from <http://www.quotationreference.com/quotefinder.php?strt=1&subj=guilt>.
[2] As quoted from <http://www.forgiver.net/reconcile.htm>.
[3] Isaiah 1:18, TLB.
[4] Psalm 38:4-8, *The Message*.
[5] Psalm 51:3, parapharased.
[6] Psalm 32:5, parapharased.
[7] Hebrews 10:22.
[8] As quoted in S. Rickly Christian, *Alive 2* (Grand Rapids, Mich.: Zondervan, 1983), 91.
[9] As quoted in *Bible Illustrator*, Parsons Technology, index 1762-1765.
[10] Isaiah 43:18, 19, TEV.
[11] As quoted from <http://www.janko.at/Zitate/EN/006.htm>.
[12] Not her real name.

CHAPTER SEVEN

Pride[1]

"Lord, when we are wrong, make us willing to change.
And when we are right, make us easy to live with."
—PETER MARSHALL

We live in a world that tends to be quite casual about the problem of pride. We're swamped with books on how to achieve wealth, beauty, happiness, and success, but there aren't many bestsellers with titles like *Seven Steps to a Less Glamorous Life* or *How to Land the Lowest Job*. Don King, the boxing promoter, captured our culture's attitude toward humility when he said, "Sometimes I amaze even my own self . . . and I say that humbly." Let's face it: Our culture is ambivalent about this humility deal.

Most of us readily admit to the problems we've addressed thus far in this book. We're quick to confess failure, anger, guilt, and so on. But pride? Few pilgrims see it as a big deal.

You need to know, however, this casual attitude toward pride is not biblical. Listen to Scripture: "The Lord preserves the faithful, but the proud he pays back in full."[2] "Whoever has haughty eyes and a proud heart, him will I not endure."[3] "God detests all the proud of heart. Be sure of this: They will not go unpunished."[4] "God opposes the proud but gives grace to the humble."[5] Or consider the punch line of our Bible study at hand: "And those who walk in pride he is able to humble."[6] Let's take a closer look at that story in Daniel, chapter four.

A portrait of pride

King Nebuchadnezzar, To the nations and peoples of ev-

94

Pride

ery language, who live in all the world: May you prosper greatly! It is my pleasure to tell you about the miraculous signs and wonders that the Most High God has performed for me. How great are his signs, how mighty his wonders! His kingdom is an eternal kingdom; his dominion endures from generation to generation. I, Nebuchadnezzar, was at home in my palace, contented and prosperous.[7]

Nebuchadnezzar acknowledges God as the source of his contentment and prosperity, but later he extols himself as the reason for his success. Let's eavesdrop on a conversation that Nebuchadnezzar has with himself. "Twelve months later, as the king was walking on the roof of the royal palace of Babylon, he said, 'Is this not the great Babylon I have built as the royal residence, by my mighty power and for the glory of my majesty?' "[8]

Notice whom Nebuchadnezzar credits now. This delusional king is not unlike the patient at a psychiatric institution. Every evening he would shout from his cell, "I am the King of the Universe! I am the Ruler of the World. Everyone will do as I say for I am the Supreme Commander of the Universe!"

You can tell whether you are becoming a servant by how you act when people treat you like one.
—GORDAN MACDONALD

One evening a doctor dropped in and confronted him. "Harry! Get down off your chair. Stop beating your chest. You're disrupting people who are trying to sleep."

"But I am the King of the Universe."

"Harry, you are not the King of the Universe."

"Yes, I am," he cried all the louder.

"And just what makes you think you are the King of the Universe?"

"*God told me* I was the King of the Universe!"

PILGRIM'S PROBLEMS

Just then a voice erupted from another cell down the hallway: "I did not!"

In my experience, it is not theology itself that causes confusion, mistrust, difficulty, and hurt in churches. It is the attitude of spiritual arrogance that accompanies it that deeply disturbs me.
—JOHN SULLIVAN

Like Nebuchadnezzar, many men have fancied themselves as God. In Nebuchadnezzar's case, he was arguably the most powerful person on the planet. His record of achievement is almost without parallel in human history.

Babylon, the capital city of his empire, was the site of so much building under Nebuchadnezzar that it takes 126 pages just to record the inscriptions that were carved into the buildings that he had constructed. The city was the site of the Hanging Gardens—touted as one of the seven wonders of the ancient world. It was protected by a double wall around it. The fifty-six-mile-long outer wall was wide enough for a four-horse chariot to pull off a U-turn. No wonder historians claim that the splendor of Babylon surpassed any city in the known world.

No wonder Nebuchadnezzar could gloat in his prosperity. He was content and prosperous. And yet he was clueless to his problem. See, one of the great dangers of pride is that people who have the biggest problem with it are the last to know.

So God presses Nebuchadnezzar onto a path that will be very long and very painful. Look at the next verse:

I had a dream that made me afraid. As I was lying in my bed, the images and visions that passed through my mind terrified me. So I commanded that all the wise men of Babylon be brought before me to interpret the dream for me. When the magicians, enchanters, astrologers and diviners came, I told them the dream, but they could not interpret it for me. Finally,

Pride

Daniel came into my presence and I told him the dream. (He is called Belteshazzar, after the name of my god, and the spirit of the holy gods is in him.)

I said, "Belteshazzar, chief of the magicians, I know that the spirit of the holy gods is in you, and no mystery is too difficult for you. Here is my dream; interpret it for me."[9]

The text goes on to describe the dream. He dreamed of a gigantic tree that housed birds and offered shelter to many animals and supplied food for a nation. But suddenly this tree gets cut down then bound in iron and bronze.

Daniel freaked out. Scripture records, "Then Daniel (also called Belteshazzar) was greatly perplexed for a time, and his thoughts terrified him. So the king said, 'Belteshazzar, do not let the dream or its meaning alarm you.' "[10]

Daniel understands the dream to be a judgment from God. Understandably, he cowers a bit in sharing the news. After all, this is a king who wasn't known for his patience and compassion. Remember, the furnace is just down the hall.

But there is one subtle thing in the story for which we must commend Nebuchadnezzar. The king knows that Daniel does not have a warm and fuzzy word from the Lord. The prophet is as stressed as a mouse at a cat convention. Nebuchadnezzar can see this; he could tell Daniel, "Only give me happy news, little prophet boy. Serve it up with a positive spin." Instead, he says to Daniel, "Tell me the truth. Don't pussyfoot around it. Just shoot straight."

God sends no one away empty except those who are full of themselves.
—DWIGHT LYMAN MOODY

Do you have someone like that in your life? Who is it that speaks truth to you regardless of the unsavory consequences? If you're hesitating to answer such questions, perhaps you should invite someone to serve you in that role.

Nebuchadnezzar wanted the truth. So Daniel interprets the dream.

Belteshazzar answered, "My Lord, if only the dream applied to your enemies and its meaning to your adversaries! The tree you saw, which grew large and strong, with its top touching the sky, visible to the whole earth, with beautiful leaves and abundant fruit, providing food for all, giving shelter to the beasts of the field, and having nesting places in its branches for the birds of the air—you, O king, are that tree! You have become great and strong. Your greatness has grown until it reaches the sky, and your dominion extends to distant parts of the earth.

"You, O king, saw a messenger, a holy one, coming down from heaven and saying, 'Cut down the tree and destroy it, but leave the stump, bound with iron and bronze, in the grass of the field, while its roots remain in the ground. Let him be drenched with the dew of heaven; let him live like the wild animals, until seven times pass by for him.' "[11]

Daniel clarifies that the king is the tree; he is a great political leader who is about to be cut down. The king has demonstrated a haughty spirit that God can no longer tolerate. Nebuchadnezzar needs to learn that he is not as great as he likes to fancy.

If ever a man becomes proud, let him remember that a mosquito preceded him in the divine order of creation.

—TALMUD

A similar, although smaller, example of this comes from the life of Richard Daly, the eccentric mayor who served in Chicago for twenty-one years. Once a speech writer approached him and requested a raise. Daly's response was, "I'm not going to give you any more money. You're getting paid enough. It should be enough for you to work for a great American hero like myself." That was the end of it—or so he thought.

Two weeks later, Daly gave a speech to honor veterans on Veterans'

Pride

Day. He was famous for not reading his speeches in advance. So there he stood before a packed house of veterans and media personnel. He spoke eloquently of the forgotten soldiers. He shared how the world had discarded this important group of people. The audience sat spellbound. "But I care. And today, I am proposing a seventeen-point program, national, state and city-wide to take care of the veterans of this country." Now, by this time, all the people were sitting on the edge of their seats. They wanted to know what the mayor would say next. Daly was pretty interested himself to find out what he would say next.

Most of the trouble in the world is caused by people wanting to be important.
—T. S. ELIOT

Turning the page, Daly saw these words: "You're on your own now, you great American hero."[12]

Nebuchadnezzar was a great Babylonian hero with unspeakable power and influence, but, like Richard Daly, he was about to be cut down to size. Look at the next verse:

> "This is the interpretation, O king, and this is the decree the Most High has issued against my lord the king: You will be driven away from people and will live with the wild animals; you will eat grass like cattle and be drenched with the dew of heaven. Seven times will pass by for you until you acknowledge that the Most High is sovereign over the kingdoms on earth and gives them to anyone he wishes. The command to leave the stump of the tree with its roots means that your kingdom will be restored to you when you acknowledge that Heaven rules."[13]

This dream captures Nebuchadnezzar's life through the metaphor of a tree. He is a towering sequoia—proud, stubborn, and self-sufficient. There is no acknowledgment on his part of dependence on God. There's no sense that one day he's going to be accountable to God, that he is a servant to God and the people of his kingdom.

Gregory the Great once said, "Pride makes me think that I am the cause of my achievements, and that I deserve my abilities, and leads me to despise other people that don't measure up."[14] Pride feeds this illusion of self-sufficiency. "I made myself. I deserve all I have."

Pastor John Ortberg tells the delightful story of a CEO at a huge corporation who showed a similar spirit of pride. One time, he was coming out of a service station only to notice his wife involved in an animated discussion with the attendant pumping their gas. Back on the road again, the CEO's wife explained how she knew the attendant. "In fact," she said, "we dated for a couple years."

After a long pause, the husband quipped, "I'll bet I know what you're thinking. I'll bet you're thinking that you're pretty lucky that you married me, the CEO of a great corporation and not a lowly service station attendant."

"No," the wife replied, "actually I was thinking if I had married him and not you, he'd be the CEO of a great corporation, and you'd be a service station attendant."

Who isn't tempted to think, "I made myself who I am"? We're all inclined to forget that every breath is a gift from God, aren't we?

Nebuchadnezzar, the great king who enjoyed unparalleled power, was about to be reminded of this problem.

A proud man is always looking down on things and people; and, of course, as long as you're looking down, you can't see something that's above you.
—C. S. Lewis

Let's return to the story. After sharing the dream and the interpretation, Daniel presses the king to repent of his sin. "Therefore, O king, be pleased to accept my advice: Renounce your sins by doing what is right, and your wickedness by being kind to the oppressed. It may be that then your prosperity will continue."[15]

Daniel could have recoiled under the pressure. He could have shared milk-toast suggestions like, "Think about your spiritual life, King."

Pride

Instead, he gets in the king's face and demands, "Do what's right." It could be translated, "Do justice," for it includes the idea of a fair distribution of resources. It is, in part, an economic term. Daniel is addressing Nebuchadnezzar's use of power and wealth.

It's ludicrous for any Christian to believe that he or she is the worthy object of public worship; it would be like the donkey carrying Jesus into Jerusalem believing the crowds were cheering and laying down their garments for him.
—CHARLES COLSON

The message is clear: "Stop your self-centered hoarding and care for the poor." Daniel is attacking Nebuchadnezzar's use of money. He's wondering how much more money is going to be spent on hanging gardens, imposing walls, and palatial estates, while the oppressed get neglected.

This exchange between Daniel and the king cuts to the heart of Christian humility, which at its core is a calling to serve people. Humility means letting go of my petty agenda, humbly receiving grace from God, and serving the people that He loves so scandalously. It's a call to notice and see and love and serve those Jesus called "the least of these."

Nebuchadnezzar, in foolish arrogance, scoffed at the invitation to practice a life of hands-on humility. He groveled like an animal for seven years until he would declare "Those who walk in pride [God] is able to humble."[16]

Hands-on humility

One way or another, Nebuchadnezzar would learn the hard lesson of hands-on humility. What does hands-on humility look like? In a verse, it is summarized like this: "Renounce your sins by doing what is right, and your wickedness by being kind to the oppressed."[17] Of course, it's a lesson that God calls you and me to learn as well.

It's a lesson God had to teach O. Frank Valladares. He's the Miami attorney who reluctantly consented to tag along with his wife on a mission trip to the Dominican Republic back in 1999. He figured the trip would be a needed vacation to escape the stresses of work and squeeze in a little scuba diving. What happened when he got there changed his life.

A doctor friend of theirs invited them to meet him at an orphanage. Frank was not prepared for what they were about to see. Listen to how Frank describes it: "I had never experienced such deplorable conditions in my life. The first thing that hit me as I walked into the orphanage was the stench of human excrement and urine, which permeated all of my clothing and even my skin, and made breathing a arduous task."[18]

The building had no running water, no air-conditioning, no working toilets, exposed electrical wiring, broken windows, deteriorating walls, and leaky ceilings. Here, seventy-five deformed, dehydrated, abandoned, starving orphans were housed.

Frank focused on an eight-year-old boy they nicknamed Cappuccino. (Nobody knew his real name.) Naked, the boy was locked in a three-foot-by-four-foot cage.

"Why is he imprisoned in there?" Frank asked.

"Well, because he is hyperactive, and that's the only way to control him," a staff person answered.

Meanwhile, his wife, Lourdes, watched a little boy afflicted with cerebral palsy dragging himself along the filthy floor with his elbows and knees. It was the only way he could move.

> *Pride is at the bottom of all great mistakes.*
> —JOHN RUSKIN

Frank describes that moment as a time when "God grabbed our hearts." No longer could Frank justify his cushy life of ease and still claim the name of Christ. He was captured by a calling to humility. Real humility. That is, humility that loves in the way the apostle John called us to when he wrote, "Let us not love with words or tongue but with actions."[19] Frank felt compelled to act.

Pride

The essential vice, the utmost evil, is pride. Unchastity, anger, greed, drunkenness, and all that, are mere fleabites in comparison. It was through pride that the devil became the devil. Pride leads to every other vice; it is the complete anti-God state of mind.

—C. S. Lewis

Following the mission trip, the Valladares family established a nonprofit Christian organization headquartered in their garage called Project ChildHelp. Their mission is to provide humanitarian help to the orphans in the Dominican Republic. Frank recruits doctors, nurses, and everybody he can to visit to help the children. Every time Frank has a vacation, he spends it taking 5,000 pounds of medicine, food, and clothes to the ones he calls "the forgotten children." American Airlines heard what Frank was doing and offered to ship all the supplies for free. And now there are kids who eat three times a day (rather than once every other day) and who get bathed every day (rather than once a month—if at all). They get touched and held and loved.

And it's all because somebody answered the call to humility and expressed love—not just in word but with actions. Frank and Lourdes were willing to put their humility into action.

How about you? How willing are you to love? Not to pay lip service to love, but life service?

If Frank's story teaches us anything, it is this: One person can make a big difference. Never underestimate the power of one humble life in the hands of God. You really can change the world through His love.

So what are you waiting for?

BRINGING IT HOME

How seriously do I take this problem of pride?

PILGRIM'S PROBLEMS

Who is the most humble person I know? What is it about this person that makes them humble?

How is God asking me to change the world?

Why does God make such a big deal out of pride?

Discuss the story of Nebuchadnezzar with a friend. Do you feel God was too harsh, too lenient, or fair with the king?

Reflect on a time when pride has tripped you up.

Make a covenant with a group of friends to practice hands-on humility.

Pray for a deeper spirit of humility.

Do a Web search and learn more about Project ChildHelp.

---

[1] I am indebted for the commentary and inspiration of this chapter to the downloaded manuscripts of John Ortberg's sermons: "Pursuing Spiritual Excellence: O Lord It's Hard to be Humble" (C0110), and "Old Testament Challenge, part 25, Amos: How God Measures a Life" (C0217), <http://www/willowcreek.org>.

[2] Psalm 31:23.

[3] Psalm 101:5.

[4] Proverbs 16:5.

[5] James 4:6.

[6] Daniel 4:37.

[7] Daniel 4:1-4.

[8] Daniel 4:29, 30.

[9] Daniel 4:5-9.

[10] Daniel 4:19.

[11] Daniel 4:19-23

[12] As quoted at <http://www.northsideaog.org/radio5_06_02.html>.

[13] Daniel 4:24-26.

[14] As quoted at <http://mns.lcms.org/gvlc/sermons/07-07-02.htm>.

[15] Daniel 4:27.

[16] Daniel 4:37.

[17] Daniel 4:27.

[18] O. Frank Valladares, "The Trip of a Lifetime," PROJECT ChildHelp, No. 1, 25 June 2000, 4.

[19] 1 John 3:18.

CHAPTER EIGHT

Fear

"Do the thing you fear and the death of fear is certain."
—RALPH WALDO EMERSON

In her book, *Effective Speaking,* Christine Stuart cites a survey in the USA where 3,000 adults were asked to list their ten worst fears. Landing at the number one spot was the fear of public speaking—eclipsing even the fear of death![1] I think about this every time I conduct a funeral. As I stand by the casket, it strikes me as strange that most folk would rather be lying in there than stand where I am.

This has been a good year for people who make money from fear. Sales of gas masks, antibiotics, concrete bunkers, tranquilizers, and lucky charms have reached all-time highs.

Barry Glassner, author of *The Culture of Fear,* suggests that "we compound our worries beyond all reason."[2] He cites the work of magazine writer Bob Garfield, who reviewed articles about serious diseases published over the course of a year in the *Washington Post,* the *New York Times,* and *USA Today.* He learned that, in addition to 59 million Americans with heart disease, 53 million with migraines, 25 million with osteoporosis, 16 million with obesity, and 3 million with cancer, many Americans suffer from more obscure ailments such as temporomandibular joint disorders (10 million) and brain injuries (2 million). Adding up the estimates, Garfield determined that 543 million Americans are seriously sick—a shocking number in a nation of 266 million inhabitants. "Either as a society we are doomed, or someone is seriously double-dipping," he suggested.[3]

Glassner suggests that the media plays a significant role in fertilizing our fears. He writes:

> In stories on topics such as school safety and childhood trauma, reporters recapitulated the gory details of the killings. And the news media made a point of reporting every incident in which a child was caught at school with a gun or making a death threat. In May, when a fifteen-year-old in Springfield, Oregon, did open fire in a cafeteria filled with students, killing two and wounding twenty-three others, the event felt like a continuation of a "disturbing trend" (*New York Times*). The day after the shooting, on National Public Radio's "All Things Considered," the criminologist Vincent Schiraldi tried to explain that the recent string of incidents did not constitute a trend, that youth homicide rates had declined by 30 percent in recent years, and more than three times as many people were killed by lightning than by violence at schools. But the show's host, Robert Siegel, interrupted him. "You're saying these are just anomalous events?" he asked, audibly peeved. The criminologist reiterated that anomalous is precisely the right word to describe the events, and he called it "a grave mistake" to imagine otherwise.[4]

Still, our fear continues to escalate. It's often fueled in our families. Growing up, we're conditioned to fear. What did your mom say to you as a little kid on your way to school? "Be careful!" It's a rare mom that says, "Take risks, honey. Embrace danger. Look just one way when you cross the street."

Fear is tax that conscience pays to guilt.
—GEORGE SEWELL

It's hard to live beyond fear, not just because we live in a culture of fear or because of our upbringing. There's a physiological component to fear as well. It turns out that there is a gene for worry (gene number SLC6A4 on chromosome number 17Q12, if you must know). People with a short version of this gene are more likely to worry than people who have a long version of it. If you're worried that you have the short version, you probably do.

It's quite clear that given our culture, our upbringing, and our wiring patterns, we will not drift into life beyond or without fear. This is nothing new. The apostle Paul was well aware of our penchant for fear rather than faith. Thus, he began his final letter to Timothy by addressing this dichotomy between fear and faith.

Fear. His modus operandi is to manipulate you with the mysterious, to taunt you with the unknown. Fear of death, fear of failure, fear of God, fear of tomorrow—his arsenal is vast. His goal? To create cowardly, joyless souls. He doesn't want you to make the journey to the mountain. He figures if he can rattle you enough, you will take your eyes off the peaks and settle for a dull existence in the flatlands.
—MAX L. LUCADO

After the customary greeting and salutation, Paul compliments Timothy's faith. "I have been reminded of your sincere faith, which first lived in your grandmother Lois and in your mother Eunice and, I am persuaded, now lives in you also."[5] Paul acknowledges a heritage now evident in Timothy. He then encourages Timothy to stoke that faith.

"For this reason I remind you to fan into flame the gift of God, which is in you through the laying on of my hands. For God did not give us a spirit of timidity, but a spirit of power, of love and of self-discipline."[6] Although your translation probably does not capitalize the word "spirit," Paul is nonetheless speaking here of the Holy Spirit. The context demonstrates that Paul is equating "sincere faith" with the presence of the Holy Spirit. Thus, Paul is teaching Timothy that "since your faith is sincere, since the Spirit of God resides in you, don't be timid; don't be paralyzed by fear."

We read on: "So do not be ashamed to testify about our Lord, or ashamed of me his prisoner. But join with me in suffering for the gospel, by the power of God, who has saved us and called us to a holy life—not because of anything we have done but because of his own purpose and grace."[7]

> *F*ear imprisons, faith liberates;
> fear paralyzes, faith empowers; fear
> disheartens, faith encourages; fear sickens,
> faith heals; fear makes useless, faith makes
> serviceable—and, most of all, fear puts
> hopelessness at the heart of life,
> while faith rejoices in its God.
> —Harry Emerson Fosdick

The faith-based life—or what Paul calls the "holy life"—must always be anchored in grace. To trust God fully is a gift; we can trust God not because of anything we do, but because of God's grace. Paul then expands this thought.

> This grace was given us in Christ Jesus before the beginning of time, but it has now been revealed through the appearing of our Savior, Christ Jesus, who has destroyed death and has brought life and immortality to light through the gospel. And of this gospel I was appointed a herald and an apostle and a teacher. That is why I am suffering as I am. Yet I am not ashamed, because I know whom I have believed, and am convinced that he is able to guard what I have entrusted to him for that day.[8]

Paul tells Timothy, "I am not ashamed of the Gospel; rather, I am assured that God can be trusted." This letter is an appeal to live a faith-based life rather than a fear-based life.

So, what is the dominant fuel in your life? Fear or faith?

There's a story about faith flying around the Internet that tells of a congregation in the foothills of the Great Smoky Mountains. Seems

Fear

the members built a new sanctuary on a piece of land willed to them by a church member. Ten days before the new church was to open, the local building inspector informed the pastor that the parking lot was inadequate for the size of the building. Until the church doubled the size of the parking lot, they would not be able to use the new sanctuary. Unfortunately the church, with its undersized lot, had used every inch of their land except for the mountain against which it had been built. In order to build more parking spaces, they would have to move the mountain out of the backyard.

Undaunted, the pastor announced the next Sunday morning that he would meet that evening with all members who had "mountain-moving faith." They would hold a prayer session asking God to remove the mountain from the backyard and to somehow provide enough money to have it paved and painted before the scheduled opening dedication service the following week. At the appointed time, twenty-four of the congregation's 300 members assembled for prayer. They prayed for nearly three hours. At ten o'clock the pastor said the final "Amen."

"We'll open next Sunday as scheduled," he assured everyone. "God has never let us down before, and I believe He'll be faithful this time too."

The next morning as he was working in his study there came a loud knock at his door. When he said, "Come in," a construction foreman appeared, removing his hard hat as he entered.

"Excuse me, Reverend. I'm from Acme Construction Company over in the next county. We're building a huge shopping mall. We need some fill dirt. Would you be willing to sell us a chunk of that mountain behind the church? We'll pay you for the dirt we remove and pave all the exposed area free of charge, if we can have it right away. We can't do anything else until we get the dirt in and allow it to settle properly."

---

*T*he cure for fear is faith.

—Norman Vincent Peale

The little church was dedicated the next Sunday as originally planned and there were far more members with "mountain-moving faith" on opening Sunday than there had been the previous week![9]

My question is this: Do miracles like that produce faith? Or could it be that faith produces miracles? That is, when we step out in faith and act on the conviction that God will move a mountain, what often follows is what many would deem a "miracle." But had we never acted on our faith, the miracle would not have occurred.

Whatever you fear (or supremely respect) the most, you will serve.
—Rebecca Manley Pippert

Simply put, the faith-based life is built on action, while the fear-based life is built on avoidance. Let's unpack that.

A fear-based life, or avoidance

The first human response to fear was avoidance. There is no record of fear in human experience until sin entered the world. After Adam disobeyed, God tracked him down in the Garden of Eden and called out, "Where are you?"

Listen to Adam's answer: "I heard you in the garden, and I was afraid because I was naked; so I hid."[10]

Adam could have confessed his sin to God. Instead he hid. Generally speaking, fear prompts people into hiding rather than into the light. Default mode for fear is to escape down avenues of avoidance. What do these avenues look like? Consider the following faces of fear.

The first face is procrastination. It looks like this: There's a phone call I need to make, but it's going to be unpleasant; it's going to involve truth-telling. Because I don't want to tackle the tough task, I keep putting it off. I hope the other person dies or moves to Mongolia so that I won't need to make the call. But, of course, life doesn't usually work out that way.

Another face of fear is denial. This attempt to avoid what I fear happens by pretending that something doesn't bother me. Or I get distracted by thinking about something else. Watching television in excess, constantly surfing the 'Net, escaping to the bottle, staying busy all the time—these are just some of the distractions that enable us to play the denial card with our fears. Our tendency toward denial would explain the line of research that shows how people who had symptoms caused by cancer were less likely to go to a doctor than people who had no symptoms at all. Why? They were afraid of the diagnosis. The irony, of course, is that the best chance of effective treatment lies in early detection, which is the one thing that is negated by denial.

Still another face of fear is indifference. You may remember a few years ago when Snoopy, the loveable beagle in the Peanuts cartoon, had his left leg broken. Hundreds wrote letters to Snoopy or sent sympathy cards. Snoopy himself philosophized about his plight one day while perched on top of his doghouse and looking at the huge white cast on his leg. "My body blames my foot for not being able to go places. My foot says it was my head's fault, and my head blamed my eyes.... My eyes say my feet are clumsy, and my right foot says not to blame him for what my left foot did...." Snoopy looks out at his audience and confesses, "I don't say anything because I don't want to get involved." That's a much easier route to take than facing our fear, isn't it? Just refuse to get involved.

Now here's the deal with avoidance: Avoidance is tempting because it promises short-term relief. But it's a long-term prison. It may stick a bandage on my anxiety, but it doesn't solve squat. Furthermore, it's a way of saying that I can't handle reality.

Skepticism is slow suicide.
—Ralph Waldo Emerson

You may remember the classic line from the movie *A Few Good Men*. Tom Cruise is interrogating Jack Nicholson on the witness chair. In total exasperation, Tom Cruise shouts, "I just want the truth." Remember Nicholson's retort? "You can't handle the truth."

Well, that's the devil's line to trap us in fear. "You can't handle the truth."

How different it is with Jesus. He promises, "Then you will know the truth, and the truth will set you free."[11] You have to decide, whom do you trust? Jesus or Jack Nicholson? "You can't handle the truth" or "You will know the truth, and the truth will set you free"? Therein is the foundation of a faith-based life. At the heart of this kind of life is action as opposed to avoidance in a fear-based life.

PILGRIM'S PROBLEMS

A faith-based life, or action

Now let's look at three faces of a faith-based life. Paul identifies these marks when he tells Timothy "God did not give us a spirit of timidity, but a spirit of power, of love and of self-discipline."[12]

First, a faith-based life is marked by a spirit of power. The Greek word here is *dunamis,* from which we get our word "dynamite." In other words, faith is an action word with power behind it. Typically, God does not remove whatever it is we fear. Nor does He erase our fears. On the contrary, He builds our faith when we embrace that fear.

To steal a phrase from my early days of skiing, we have to "lean into the mountain." This was the first lesson I ever learned on the slopes.

Skiing sounded easy, although I couldn't see the sense in paying an arm and a leg to break an arm and a leg, I listened to my cousin Danny. "It's a no-brainer," he said. "Anybody with an IQ higher than a jar of mustard can ski." Before he left me to my demise, he pumped me up with a pep talk. He said, "You'll figure it out, but there is just one thing you need to remember: Lean into the mountain."

"OK!" I chirped. "Lean into the mountain. Right on! …Huh?"

Danny explained how I'd need to fight the natural inclination to lean back. Instead, I should attack my fear and lean forward. With that advice he disappeared. I didn't see him until the slopes closed that night.

I shuffled in the lift line. Unfortunately, I moved faster than the line. Are you familiar with the domino theory? I squeaked from the bottom of the pile of skiers, "Who fell?"

I don't possess a lot of self-confidence. I'm an actor so I simply act confident every time I hit the stage. I am consumed with the fear of failing. Reaching deep down and finding confidence has made all my dreams come true.

—ARSENIO HALL

The ski lift churned up. And up. And up. Off to my left was the famous New Hampshire landmark, The Old Man on the Mountain.

Fear

To my right I could see Mount Kilimanjaro. (You can see a lot from the top of the world!)

Getting off the ski lift wasn't any easier. How was I to know I was supposed to get off *before* the chair curled to reverse direction? Unfortunately, an astute lift attendant noticed I was safely heading down the mountain and alertly stopped the chairs and commanded, "Jump."

"Jump?" I echoed in disbelief. "Get me a bungee cord and we'll talk."

"Jump! Now!"

I slid to the edge of my seat. Closing my eyes, I lunged forward and dropped like a shot duck. I landed in front of a sign displaying a large black diamond with the name of the run: The Devil's Vomit. I peered over the edge like a cat wanting off the roof of the Trump Tower.

All forms of fear produce fatigue.
—BERTRAND RUSSELL

An hour later I was thirty feet down the mountain—only because I was wearing slippery clothing. Finally, I summoned the courage to try Danny's advice and lean into the mountain. I leaned forward and clocked in at mach ten. I had to keep a keen eye out for small children . . . so they could break my fall.

Not really.

Here's the deal: In skiing and in life, you've got to lean into the mountain. God generally says to His frightened children, "You must face your fear head-on. You will never grow otherwise. So attack it with a keg of dynamite." Faith is an action word—it denotes power.

The second mark of a faith-based life is love. Here again, this is an action word. In his book *Mere Christianity*, C. S. Lewis wrote, "Do not waste your time bothering whether you 'love' your neighbor; act as if you did. As soon as we do this, we find one of the great secrets. When you are behaving as if you loved someone, you will presently come to love him."[13] Love is a behavior that marks the lives of faith-based people.

The third mark that Paul mentions is self-discipline. Here again is the idea of choice. It is an action word. Fear is an emotion, while discipline, or faith, is an action.

PILGRIM'S PROBLEMS

Every time you face your fear and discipline yourself to hit it head on, you bolster your belief that you and God can handle anything. That's how faith gets built. Conversely, if you opt to avoid the issue, God cannot do His work in you.

So here's an assignment: Identify one area in your life where you have been troubled by worry or fear. Then decide on one step that you can take toward constructively addressing this problem. Maybe it means making a phone call, or writing a letter, or learning something—whatever it is, do it!

When I think of us human beings, it seems to me that we have a lot of nerve to make fun of the ostrich.
—HEYWOOD BROUN

Maybe you received a grade that you didn't deserve for a class. The Holy Spirit is asking you to make it right. But you're afraid. What if you have to take the class over? What if your professor knocks your grade? What if the truth leaks out and your reputation is tarnished? You need the "A" to get into grad school. Exercise discipline and do what is right. Walk the way of faith rather than caving into your fears. Act! Don't avoid.

Maybe your fear involves a relationship. You haven't said anything to your spouse because you're afraid of the pain and conflict, of the whole mess that may result. Maybe God is saying, "You need to talk." Maybe it's a conflict with a roommate or a longtime friend. Will you decide, what is one step· that could be taken? And will you do it? Nobody can do that for you. But it will release the power of God in your life through faith in a way that nothing else will.

Maybe you're worried about an addictive behavior in your life, and the evil one is whispering, "It'll never get better. Just keep it hidden." You've been hiding, and your biggest fear has been getting caught. God's calling you now, "Come on. Take a step toward the light."

I have a friend who has been shackled with sexual addictions his whole adult life. This is what he said to me: "I've tried bungee jumping and hang gliding. I've taken financial risks that would make your fingernails sweat.

114

Fear

But the scariest risk I've ever taken was the time I walked into a Christian support group and confessed, 'I'm George, and I'm a sex addict.' "

I wonder what would have happened to him if he hadn't done that. His secret could have destroyed his soul. It could have wrecked his family and kept him trapped in deception. But it all came down to this: Would one man have enough courage to take the single step that frightened him more than anything else? Because he did, it set in motion the power of God to bring healing, restoration, and the building up of his faith in amazing ways.

As you commit to taking that hard step of faith, let me arm you with a children's prayer to take with you. A young girl was afraid to walk next door to her grandpa's house because it involved going through a field of tall grass. The girl was frightened because she harbored unrealistic fears about the dangers of monsters and wild animals and boogeymen that she believed were lurking in the field.

Her father assured her that God would be with her. "Don't fear," he encouraged, "Jesus is a real person. He'll really be with you. You won't be alone in this. He's with you all the time—even in that scary field."

"Really?" the girl wanted to be sure.

"Yes, no kidding, He really is."

Suddenly she perked up and quipped, "OK, then. I'm going to Grandpa's. Come on, Jesus."

It's that simple. God is calling you to face your fear—to walk through whatever frightening field you have in your life. When you start walking in that direction, you'll be tempted to foster destructive thoughts. Instead of feeding your doubts, pray this prayer: "Come on, Jesus."

God's never missed the runway through all the centuries of fearful fog.
—CHARLES R. SWINDOLL

There is nothing that you and God cannot handle together. He assures you, "I'll be with you. You'll walk through the waters and not be destroyed. You'll walk through fire and not get burned. You'll walk through the field and not be mugged. I am with you always."

So step out in faith. You'll never regret it.

PILGRIM'S PROBLEMS

BRINGING IT HOME

Would my friends characterize me primarily as a person of fear or faith? Why?

What is my deepest fear? Why?

When have I really trusted God? When have I demonstrated a lack of trust?

Why does God require me to have faith?

What is my preferred avenue of avoidance? How does that compromise my faith?

Think about the most trustworthy person you know. Analyze what it is specifically that makes them trustworthy.

List the attributes you most admire in each person mentioned in Hebrews 11, the faith chapter.

Do something today for someone else that can only be explained by your total trust in God.

Write your definition of faith and display it on your computer's screen saver.

---

[1] As quoted from <http://www.bradford.ac.uk/acad/civeng/skills/pubspeak.htm>.

[2] As quoted from <http://www.bowlingforcolumbine.com/library/fear/index.php>.

[3] Ibid.

[4] Ibid.

[5] 2 Timothy 1:5.

[6] 2 Timothy 1:6, 7.

[7] 2 Timothy 1:8, 9.

[8] 2 Timothy 1:9-12.

[9] Author unknown. As quoted from <http://www.servingthelord.com/Miracles/faith.htm>.

[10] Genesis 3:10.

[11] John 8:32.

[12] 2 Timothy 1:7.

[13] C. S. Lewis, *Mere Christianity,* p. 116, as quoted at <http://www.harpercollins.com/catalog/guide_xml.asp?isbn=0060652926>.

CHAPTER NINE

Greed

*"The more you have to live for, the less you need
to live on. Those who make acquisition their goal
never have enough."*
—SYDNEY HARRIS

She has been dubbed "The Poster Child for Greed." Leona Helmsley owns and operates fourteen high-end hotels, the Empire State Building, and several other properties in New York City. In September 1989, she was convicted of thirty-three counts of tax evasion. When declaring the verdict, Judge John Walker said, "Your conduct was the product of naked greed." He then sentenced Helmsley to four years in prison—of which she served eighteen months—and 750 hours of community service and $7.1 million in fines.

According to *Time* magazine, Helmsley emerged as a "penny-pinching tyrant who tried to stiff just about everybody. No amount of money was too small to fight over. After the sudden death of her only son at age 40 in 1982, she sued and won the lion's share of his estate, $149,000, leaving his four children with $432 each and his widow with $2,171."[1]

Remember the eighties when greed was chic? Many people bought into the notion that "greed is good." In light of corporate scandals ranging from Enron to Martha Stewart, clearly we have not yet overcome this problem of greed. In fact, Alan Greenspan recently made this observation before the U.S. Senate committee: "It is not that humans have become any more greedy than in generations past. It is that the avenues to express greed [have] grown so enormously."[2] It's true, isn't it? The avenues to express greed are all around us.

While it's easy to recognize greed in New York property tycoons or crooked corporate executives, it's not as easy to admit that it's a big deal in the church, right?

Most ordinary situations can be experienced as deliciously pleasurable, or as bitterly disappointing. It depends on how you evaluate them. The more you are enslaved by your desires, the more likely you are to find any given situation disappointing.

—Timothy Ray Miller

Robert Wuthnow, a sociologist at Princeton University, in his book, *God and Mammon in America,* claims there is little difference in the financial behavior of those who are inside the church, as opposed to those who are outside the church. He says that according to recent surveys, 86 percent of people in America agree that greed is sin. Interestingly enough, only 16 percent of those inside the church believe that wanting a lot more money is wrong. Furthermore, four-fifths of all people who responded said that they wished that they had a lot more money, which leaves us in a quandary that the vast majority of Christians agree that greed is wrong, and yet they say, "I am not greedy, I just want a lot more money." According to Wuthnow's research, that's the prevailing attitude in the church.[3]

You may remember the cartoon portraying the Christian singer "ministering" at a piano. The caption reads: "I'd like to share a song with you that the Lord gave me a year ago—and even though he did give it to me, any reproduction of this song in any form without my written consent will constitute infringement of copyright laws, which grants me the right to sue your pants off. Praise God...."

Greed can affect us all. No wonder Jesus taught more about money than any other single topic. Nearly half His parables deal with money. So let's consult the teachings of Christ for a perspective on greed.

Matthew 6 records the Sermon on the Mount when Jesus said this: "Do not store up for yourselves treasures on earth, where moth and rust destroy, and where thieves break in and steal."[4] In essence,

Greed

Jesus is warning, "Don't build your life around stuff, because stuff is vulnerable. Cotton may be the fabric of our lives, but it also makes tasty moth food." The Greek word for moth is *nordos*—from which we get our word "Nordstrom." (OK, John Ortberg made that up, but wouldn't it be a cool coincidence if that were true? Actually, synthetic fibers are moth-resistant—so I guess the Bible is pro-polyester!)

And of course, other stuff will rust. Recently I was in New York City with a friend. We stayed in a hotel right across from Manhattan Motorcars, Inc. On display were a number of Rolls Royces and Bentleys. One Bentley Azure displayed a price tag of $300,000. And it was used. Can you imagine? That's more money than I make in an entire month. Moreover, the car didn't even have cup holders. "One day," Jesus says, "it's going to be a pile of rust." Ten thousand years from now, nobody is going to approach you in heaven and ask, "What kind of rust is your pile? Ha ha! You got a Kia pile, but mine's genuine *Mercedes* rust."

In light of the moth problem and the rust potential for stuff, Jesus goes on to offer this advice: "But store up for yourselves treasures in heaven, where moth and rust do not destroy, and where thieves do not break in and steal. For where your treasure is, there your heart will be also."[5]

---

*Y*ou can have your cake and eat it;
the only trouble is you get fat.
—Julian Barnes

The ancient Jews were familiar with the phrase "treasures in heaven." The listeners would have known of King Monobaz of Adiabene. This king was a convert to Judaism. He became famous during a time of extreme famine when he distributed all of his enormous wealth to the poor. This gesture infuriated his brothers. They cornered the king and said: "Thy fathers gathered treasures, and added to those of their fathers, but thou hast dispersed yours and theirs."

King Monobaz replied, "My fathers gathered treasures for below, I have gathered treasures for above; …my fathers gathered treasures in this world, I have gathered treasures for the world to come."[6]

Jesus was affirming the life philosophy of King Monobaz. He then uses this metaphor: "The eye is the lamp of the body. If your eyes are good, your whole body will be full of light. But if your eyes are bad, your whole body will be full of darkness. If then the light within you is darkness, how great is that darkness!"[7]

The eye is the window that lets light into one's heart and soul. If a window is dirty or frosted or distorted, the light will be hindered and the room will be dark. On the other hand, if the window is clean the light will pour into the room. The amount of light that gets into a room depends on the condition of the window through which the light needs to pass. So then Jesus says that the light that gets into a person's heart and soul depends on the spiritual state of the eye through which it has to pass, for the eye is the window of the whole body.

So ask yourself: What is the condition of my eye? Is my worldview broad enough to see the needs of people around me? Can I focus on others and invest my money to help them? Be careful before you respond because your answers reveal the condition of your soul.

Jesus then hits the punch line. "No one can serve two masters. Either he will hate the one and love the other, or he will be devoted to the one and despise the other. You cannot serve both God and Money."[8] You cannot live a life of greed and grace. You cannot serve both God and money. You must decide. Will you orient your life around matters of eternal significance or will you waste your life pursing the trivial?

Jesus taught that it is possible to store up treasures in heaven while on earth. We really can overcome greed. How? Here are three suggestions.

Often people attempt to live their lives backwards: they try to have more things, or more money, in order to do more of what they want so they will be happier. The way it actually works is the reverse. You must first be who you really are, then, do what you need to do, in order to have what you want.

—MARGARET YOUNG

Greed

Practice thanks-living

Jesus invites us to a life of contentment. Don't get sucked into the misguided notion that more stuff will make you happy. Instead, be thankful for what you already enjoy. Be mindful of your blessings every day. Such is the secret of happiness.

The evil in our desires typically does not lie in what we want, but that we want it too much.

—JOHN CALVIN

Sports Illustrated columnist Rick Reilly asked some of the world's greatest athletes this simple question: When were you happiest? Now you might expect the athletes to recall some great victory or major paycheck or athletic accomplishment. Ironically, nearly every athlete spoke not about achievements, but rather, they spoke of significant relationships. Listen to a sampling:

Jack Nicklaus: "Probably the day Barbara called and said, 'You're a daddy!' I was playing in a tournament in Cincinnati, but when I got to the hospital in Columbus, I said, 'Which one's mine?' They pointed to Jackie, and I fainted straight away. I passed out when all my kids were born. I learned to bring a pillow and smelling salts."

Martina Navratilova: "It was when I was nine, living in Prague with my grandmother. She would bring me sliced carrot salad so I could see the ball better. She didn't own a TV. We'd do crossword puzzles and listen to the radio. I was her golden little girl. She saw me play once in Dallas and passed away not long after that. I can never have those years back."

Tiger Woods: "I was 11. I got straight A's, had two recesses a day, had the cutest girlfriend and won 32 tournaments. Everything's been downhill since."

Kurt Warner: "It wasn't the Super Bowl season; it was two years before that. I got married, we got pregnant, and I got signed by the Rams. I remember Brenda and I had finally scraped up enough money to buy a house together, so we went out to a nice dinner. While we were out, I had a buddy come and throw rose petals on our walk. I had written WILL YOU MARRY ME? in Christmas lights on the house. Then I turned to her two kids and said, 'Will you all marry me?' and they all said, 'Yes.' "[9]

Before we set our hearts too much upon anything, let us examine how happy they are who already possess it.

—FRANCOIS DE LA ROCHEFOUCAULD

Notice the theme in their stories. It seems that happiness is connected to community. Happiness is directly proportional to the quality of our relationships, not the quantity of money in our bank accounts. To practice thanks-living, be aware of these blessings each day.

I got a personal reminder to do this when a friend, Linda, called the other day. "Hey Karl," she said, "can you park your car again in the Alumni Antique Car Show?"

"Sure," I said, "assuming I can crank the handle fast enough and get it started. I haven't driven it since the show last year."

Although the comment about getting it started was only a joke, when I tried to fire it up, I wasn't laughing. The engine coughed, then went quiet. It would only be coaxed alive by cables. Even so, the dashboard stubbornly illuminated the warning, "Gen."

Having the mechanical aptitude of J. Lo, I called my friend Dallas. "I'm on my way to Big Cheese Pizza. I'm driving the Ford because I wanted to run it through the carwash before the show this weekend, but it wouldn't start. I jumpstarted it but now the generator light is on. You think that's a problem?"

"You're probably OK," Dallas replied.

The six-mile trip to the other side of town provided ample time to ponder my problems. *This car is a pain. It's a maintenance nightmare, a heap of junk, a useless boat that hogs space in the garage. I need to sell it. What if the generator light stays on forever?*

Greed

My carping continued until I arrived at the Big Cheese drive-through. When the kid working the window saw me, he leaned forward and gasped, "Whoooooooooa!"

"I'm here to pick up two olive pizzas for Haf—"

"A '64, isn't it?"

"Huh?" The kid confused me. By now he was hanging out the window as if he was about to upchuck.

"This is the XL Galaxie with the leather interior and electric seats, right?"

"What? Oh, the car? Uh, yeah, my grandpa bought it new. It's always been kept in a garage."

"You are soooooo lucky. That's got the 391 under the hood, doesn't it?"

"Um, ah, yeah . . . a 391, 392, 393 . . . something like that."

For five minutes the kid rattled off numbers about my car that only Ford engineers who get paid mountains of money should know. I was waiting for him to recite the VIN.

"I'm restoring a '72 Impala right now, but it's nothing like *your* car."

I couldn't think of what to say (except maybe, "Could you get my stinkin' pizza before it freezes!"). I could only marvel at his marveling.

Next, I went to the carwash. While the suds swirled around me, the recent conversation echoed in my mind.

It is a nice car, I mused. My mind detoured through many chapters of my childhood with the "Ole' Gal." I thought of Grandpa piling us into the Ford to hit the A&W store. I remembered playing for hours with the electric seats. I smiled at the memory of my brothers stumping everyone when they hid in the Ford's trunk during a game of hide-and-seek.

Money doesn't change men, it merely unmasks them. If a man is naturally selfish or arrogant or greedy, the money brings that out, that's all.

—HENRY FORD

Then I thought of college days. My first date with Cherié, our honeymoon, our first kiss (not necessarily in that order), all happened in the Ford. Suddenly I was consumed in a world of nostalgia.

Had someone approached me in that moment and said, "I'll give you a million dollars for your car," you know what I'd have said?

"Show me the money!"

I mean, it's a nice car and all, but with a million bucks I could always buy another one.

My greed notwithstanding, I did think about how easy it is to skimp in the thankfulness department. Hearing someone else's perspective reminded me of a blessing I enjoy.

Whether it's a Christian education, a trusted friend, a warm house, or a ripe peach, it's easy to take these and a billion other blessings for granted.

So open your eyes and thank God for the luxuries of life. You may just see things you hadn't noticed before. (By the way, when I finally opened my eyes in the carwash, I noticed the generator light was off!)

Be content

Another ingredient of a greedless life is contentment. Whether you own a small empire like Leona or you've got a lot less, be content with what you have.

The apostle Paul has something to teach us in this department. I maintain that he was content because he never bought shoes. If he did, it was *after* writing Philippians 4:11: "I have learned to be content." You can't be content when you're buying shoes.

Visit any shoe store. Notice the music that's playing. Next, listen to it backwards. Hear the message? "Buy a dozen pairs lest thee be an idiot—lest thee be an idiot—lest thee be an idiot...."

---

*A*nyway, no drug, not even alcohol, causes
the fundamental ills of society. If we're
looking for the source of our troubles,
we shouldn't test people for drugs;
we should test them for stupidity,
ignorance, greed and love of power.
—P. J. O'ROURKE

I'm aware of this backmasking technique because last night I was shopping for a pair of running shoes. I picked out a pair that was

Greed

identical to a Boeing 747 in cost, except the shoes were much more technologically sophisticated. The Reeboks came with air-bags and a pump. The orthopedic benefit of this advanced air-system is simple: It allows the manufacturer to pump up the price.

While I was admiring the pair of sneakers, a salesman moseyed my direction. "Looking to invest in a pair of *shoes?*" he asked.

"Yeah, um, just a pair of running shoes," I said.

"Then why are you looking at *that pair?*" He looked at me as though I needed to see a therapist before my next heartbeat. "*That pair* is not for running. Those are jogging shoes. Our running shoes are over here."

I have news for the forces of greed
and the defenders of the status quo:
your time has come—and gone.
It's time for change in America.
—William Jefferson Clinton

We hiked to the opposite side of the super-store—which was conveniently located in a different county. "Now here are running shoes," he said. "Look at this pair. They're on sale for $149.99."

He explained how the sneakers were as comfortable as bare feet. If that's the case, and I know this is a stupid question, but why wouldn't you take off the shoes and save the hundred and fifty bucks?

"I dunno," I said. "For the little bit of walking I do—"

"Walking? Then you need walking shoes too. Follow me."

I wanted to tell the guy to take a hike, but then he would have dragged me to the hiking boots. There was no way around the fact that unless I took out a second mortgage, I would die from insufficient sneakerage. At least that's what the salesman wanted me to believe.

On the other foot, the apostle Paul wants me to believe the opposite. He claims we can be happy without running shoes, karate shoes, volleyball shoes, flirting shoes, and cell-phone-technology shoes. According to him, we can be content in bare feet. And he ought to know. After all, he never bought shoes.

PILGRIM'S PROBLEMS

Live to give

One more suggestion: Cultivate the habit of generosity. Consider the story of John D. Rockefeller, Sr. At the age of twenty-three the guy was a millionaire. By fifty, he was a billionaire and dubbed the "richest man in the world."

But Rockefeller was a miserable rich man. In his quest to amass a fortune, he sacrificed his health. At fifty-three, his body was riddled with disease and ulcers. Doctors gave him less than a year to live. At the root of his ill health was Rockefeller's attitude. He was a very greedy man. His all-consuming greed proved destructive. The man who could buy any restaurant in the world with pocket change was limited to a diet of milk and crackers.

During that crisis, John D. Rockefeller reevaluated his life. He concluded, "I have all these possessions and yet I've never been a giver." That's when he decided to give much of it away. He gave to churches, hospitals, and medical research. Why not? He was going to die in a year anyway. What good would all his money do him then? Why not invest in something that would outlive him?

Today, many significant discoveries in medicine are the result of money given by the Rockefeller Foundation. Most significant, however, was the healing impact Rockefeller's giving had on him. When he focused on giving rather than getting, his health dramatically improved. His generosity proved therapeutic. John D. Rockefeller lived to the age of ninety. Along the way, he discovered that giving is a key ingredient for a life of significance.

Seems Leona Helmsley is discovering the same thing. Shortly after being released from jail, her name showed up on the Honorable Mentions list of the largest American charitable contributions of 1997. Her name continues to surface with offerings like a more recent $5 million check to the New York Police and Fire Widows' and Children's Benefit Fund. While Leona has certainly battled the demon of greed, it appears that she is discovering how to overcome this menacing monster.

You and I can overcome the monster as well. Let's just hope we don't have to learn this lesson in jail.

BRINGING IT HOME

Who is the most content person I know? Why?

Greed

How might I be tempted to believe the American model of success?

What would it look like for me to store up treasures in heaven today?

"When were you the happiest?" After reflecting on this question, interview others and reflect on their answers.

Write a definition of success based on Joshua 1:7, 8. Post it somewhere so you can read it often.

Pray that God would help you to discern the things that truly matter.

Discuss this question with your friends: "Would your death leave the world poorer, or just less crowded?"

Go to the Web site www.ask.com and type in the question: "How can I be a success?"

Look for opportunities to practice thanks-living today.

Use this week to experiment with the positive effects of giving and discover what it took Rockefeller fifty-three years to learn.

---

[1] As quoted from <http://www.christianglobe.com/Illustrations/theDetails.asp?whichOne=g&whichFile=greed>.

[2] Alan Greenspan testifying before a U.S. Senate committee, July 16, 2002, as reported in *Fast Company,* December, 2002.

[3] As quoted by John Ortberg, "What Jesus Really Taught About Greed" (South Barrington, Ill.: Seeds Tape Ministry, a ministry of Willow Creek Community Church, 1995). (R. Wuthnow,. *God and Mammon in America* (New York: The Free Press, 1995).

[4] Matthew 6:19.

[5] Matthew 6:20, 21.

[6] William Barclay, *The Daily Study Bible Series: The Gospel of Matthew* (Philadelphia: Westminster Press, 1975), 1:241.

[7] Matthew 6:22, 23.

[8] Matthew 6:24.

[9] Rick Reilly, "It Doesn't Get Any Better," *Sports Illustrated,* 20 August 2001, 84.

CHAPTER TEN

Futility

"The purpose of life is to live a life of purpose."
—RICHARD LEIDER

Mention the problem of futility and the first story that comes to my mind is an adaptation of the Creation story written by Ann Herbert that I heard back when Reagan was president. Thanks to some dazzling search engines these days, I found it on the Internet in a matter of a few keystrokes. Here's one version of it:

> In the beginning, God didn't make just two people; He made a whole bunch of us because he wanted us to have a lot of fun, and He said you can't really have fun unless there's a whole gang of you. He put us in the Garden of Eden—a combination garden and playground and park and God told us to have fun. And at first we did have fun, just like God expected us to. We rolled down the hills, waded in the streams, climbed on the trees, swung on the vines, ran in the meadows, frolicked in the woods, hid in the forest, and acted silly. We laughed a lot.
>
> Then one day this snake told us that we weren't having real fun because we weren't keeping score. Back then we didn't know what score was. When he explained it, we still couldn't see the fun of it. But then he said we should give an apple to the person who was best at all the games; and that we'd never know who was best without keeping score. Well, we

could all see the fun of that, of course, because we were all sure we were best; and second, because we were all pretty sure that apples would be a pretty tasty reward for proving it.

Life in the Garden was different after that. We yelled a lot.

We had to make up new scoring rules for most of the games. Some games, like frolicking, we stopped playing altogether because they were too hard to score.

By the time God found out what had happened we were spending about 45 minutes a day actually playing and the rest of the time working out the scoring. God was wroth about that—very, very wroth. God was so wroth, in fact, He said we couldn't use His garden anymore because we weren't having fun. We told Him we were having lots of fun. He was just being narrow-minded because it wasn't exactly the kind of fun He had originally thought of.

God would not listen. He kicked us out, and He said we couldn't come back until we stopped keeping score. And then, to rub it in (to "get our attention," He said), God told us that we were all going to die and our scores wouldn't mean anything anyway.

But let me tell you. God was wrong. My cumulative, all-game score now is 44,675—and that means a lot to me. If I can raise that score to, say, 60,000 before I die, I'll know that I've really accomplished something. And even if I can't, my life has a great deal of meaning because I've taught my children to score high and they'll be able to reach 60,000 easy, or maybe even 100,000![1]

Housework is a treadmill from futility to oblivion with stop-offs at tedium and counter-productivity.
—ERMA LOUISE BOMBECK

Sound familiar? How often do we get sucked into piling up the points, which in the end prove pointless? I can think of lots of ways we keep score—degrees, cars, boats, vacations, earrings, and a handicap at the country club—to name a few. But what's the point? Is there any meaning in this or does meaning come through some other avenue?

To answer that, let's return to the Creation story and consider what I call "the ten most important words ever written." Just one sentence—and the world has never been the same.

To appreciate the impact of these ten words, first you have to envision the ancient world when they were written. Imagine that you had never heard about a personal God who created you and loves you. Imagine that everyone believed in many gods and all these gods were limited in power. The gods were morally inept. They were petty and jealous of each other. That was the dominant mind-set of the day.

> *How strange is the lot of us mortals!*
> *Each of us is here for a brief sojourn;*
> *for what purpose he knows not,*
> *though he senses it. But without deeper*
> *reflection one knows from daily life that*
> *one exists for other people.*
> —ALBERT EINSTEIN

The result was a world where people lived in fear. They swallowed superstitions that suggested the stars had influence over the affairs of human beings (imagine that!). They worshiped objects like the sun and moon. They formed fertility cults that practiced gross sexual immorality. They sacrificed babies, hoping to manipulate their selfish and insecure gods. They scorned the value of human life and thought that people were created to do the work that the gods didn't want to mess with. It's no wonder that human beings were called the "lackeys of the gods."

The core belief in this ancient world was that life was just an endless cycle, what you might call a wheel of life rotating around the hub of death. And it was believed that generations come and go without any meaning or purpose. There was no ultimate destiny that was shaping history. There was no source of authority. Consequently, life was considered to be short, cheap, cruel, and hopeless.

Suddenly, in the context of this destructive belief system, the author of Genesis penned these words that would change the world forever: "In the beginning God created the heavens and the earth" (Genesis 1:1).

Futility

Because of that one statement, you can make sense of life. You can know that there is a supreme God who created you to be His personal friend. You did not come from a monkey or an accidental big bang in the universe. You came from the hand of the one and only supreme God, who longs to be connected to you.

Listen to how Jody and Dan Mayhew put it: "Human beings have an innate need to be connected. Without this connection, we have no direction in our lives. The proper connection for us is to find ourselves tied securely to God, our Creator, in willing and voluntary subjection to His will. The key word is voluntary. If our obedience to God is not voluntary, then we're nothing but robots. As individuals with choice, our obedience is meaningful and purpose-driven."[2]

Isn't it comforting to know that you can craft a life that is "meaningful and purpose-driven"? You don't have to be duped by a world that suggests the earth is a random mishap and your life an accidental fluke. God knows you. He loves you. And He calls you to a life of purpose.

How then do you enter into this kind of life? Consider these suggestions.

Concentrate on character

If you don't have a strong, moral character, beware! You're going to get lost in life. Listen to David's prayer for direction: "Show me your ways, O Lord, teach me your paths; guide me in your truth and teach me, for you are God my Savior."[3]

Interstate 495, which is the beltway around Washington, D.C., was clogged. I sat in my Avis rental car thinking about how nice it is to live in Walla Walla, where the only traffic jam occurs at Dairy Queen when the Peanut Buster Parfait goes on sale.

Joy is the holy fire that keeps our purpose warm and our intelligence aglow.
—HELEN KELLER

Suddenly I heard a voice from on high. "Excuse me," he said, "um, sir?"

I looked out the passenger window to see an appliance delivery truck from Sears. The driver, a dead ringer for former football player

131

William "The Refrigerator" Perry, said, "Excuse me. Do you know if this highway goes to Bethesda?"

"I don't know," I replied. "I'm from Washington."

He was clearly confused. "Yeah, so? You should know!"

"Ah, no," I said (I was just catching on!), "I'm from *Walla Walla, Washington*. I'm not from Washington, D.C."

"So does this take me into Bethesda?" He was unrelenting.

"I don't know, sir. I'm not from this area."

Then he asked me a question that still makes me chuckle. "Oh, well," he stammered, "what's your hunch?"

Now I ask you: What difference does my hunch make? It's not like the town will suddenly relocate based on my hunch. As if the residents might conspire, "Karl wants this town to be on his way from Baltimore to Shenandoah Valley Academy, so what do you say we accommodate him and move?" Bethesda is wherever Bethesda is, and my hunch isn't going to change that.

So I reiterated, "Sir, I really don't know."

"But what do you think?"

Exasperated, I finally just spouted what he wanted to hear. "Yeah, this road heads toward Bethesda. Just go on up here and you'll see the signs. Can't miss them."

"Thank you, sir!" His front gold tooth glimmered in the sunshine.

"No problem," I said as I changed lanes. Since he was about 250 pounds my senior, I didn't want him following me in case my directions were skewed!

That conversation still baffles me. Why would you ask for a stranger's *opinion* when it comes to direction? After all, there is a true north that doesn't change with a hunch.

A faith to live by, a self to live with, and a purpose to live for.
—Bob Harrington

And yet how many people live with that mind-set? They drift based on opinion rather than fact, believing there are no unchanging principles.

Futility

No wonder futility is an epidemic these days. Consider the findings of two national surveys conducted by Barna Research, one among adults and one among teenagers. People were asked if they believe in moral absolutes that are unchanging. By a 3-to-1 ratio, adults said truth is always relative to the person and their situation. The perspective looks even more skewed among teenagers: 83 percent said moral truth depends on the circumstances, and only 6 percent said moral truth is absolute.[4]

The secret of success is constancy of purpose.
—BENJAMIN DISRAELI

Well, call me old-fashioned, but I believe there is such a thing as moral truth, right and wrong, good and evil. The foundation stones for a life beyond futility have always been the same. Integrity, courage, service, responsibility, loyalty, persistence, compassion—these are but a few of the unchanging virtues that constitute a person of character. And in the end, that person will enjoy an adventure beyond futility. If you don't believe me, ask a mature Christian for a second opinion. Just don't ask some bewildered, big guy roaming aimlessly on I-495. I have a hunch he's not in a good mood.

Look beyond yourself

The most futile way to live is by always thinking "Me first." If your worldview is no bigger than your little world, futility is inevitable. Scripture teaches, "It is more blessed to give than to receive."[5]

A few years ago I filed a snapshot in my mind that continues to remind me of how unsightly selfishness is. Early that morning the telephone startled me awake. "Huh, um, hello?" I croaked.

"Sorry to wake you, buddy. I know it's early, but today's the day!"

"Really?" Suddenly I was awake.

Within three minutes I was racing south on Interstate 405. No way was I going to miss this sale at Nordstrom.

Mind you, this was no ordinary sale. It wasn't available at all stores—only at an obscure Nordstrom Rack in the Tukwila Mall. Nor was it advertised. The only way to score on this jackpot was by getting a tip from an employee at the Nordstrom administrative office.

> *The only true happiness comes from squandering ourselves for a purpose.*
> —JOHN MASON BROWN

The reputation of the sale was as legendary as the Loch Ness monster. I had heard the tales, but wouldn't believe them until I experienced the sale for myself. As the stories went, you could buy top-quality clothes for the cost of a button. Friends showed me fifty-dollar Nordstrom dress shirts they purchased new for one dollar at this sale. Five-hundred-dollar suits were twenty bucks. Polo dress pants and shirts snatched for a cool two dollars. This was no ho-hum sale.

Arriving an hour early, I joined the small posse of people huddled by the front of the store. "Good morning," I said to the woman next to me.

Too focused to acknowledge my greeting, she stared intently into the store. The store looked like a shopaholic's poster of heaven—endless tables supporting mountains of sale items.

Glancing to the woman on my left I said, "How are you today?"

Again, it was like talking to a mannequin.

Fifteen minutes before opening, a large crowd milled outside of the store.

Ten minutes before opening, the people pressed against the gated entrance.

Five minutes before showtime, I elbowed for position.

At exactly 7:00 A.M. the gate began to rise. Both women who sandwiched me into this melee got on all fours and crawled furiously under the rising gate. These were women who were decked out in business suits. These were women who vote for the President of the United States of America. These were women who need therapy!

When I finally clawed my way to a table I noticed the women again. This time, they were engaged in a tug-of-war with a leather jacket.

"I had it first," the one lady screamed. "It's mine!"

"Is not!" the other countered. "Give it to me!"

Futility

One woman planted her foot on the table for improved leverage, thus exposing a bruised thigh. It was a nasty sight so I tried not to look, but I couldn't help myself. Meanwhile, the other lady launched a verbal assault more profane than something you'd hear at a cursers' convention.

The battle boiled until security guards arrived and manhandled both women to the exit. It felt like a polluted episode of the Jerry Springer Show.

Meanwhile, the sale items quickly evaporated. I grabbed my share and replaced my wardrobe for under a hundred bucks. The sale was worth it.

But that snapshot of selfishness is forever tattooed in my mind. Two women, acting like two-year-olds: "It's mine!" "No it's not! The jacket belongs to me!"

"Me! Me! Me!" You, too, can live that way, but it's a dismal way to go. Jesus showed us a better way. He called His followers to recklessly give of themselves and their resources. By modeling the generosity of Jesus we enter into the adventure of His kingdom. We discover that it really is better to give than to receive.

I think of this lesson every time I don my leather jacket. (Except for the claw marks on the arms, it's still in decent shape.) At five bucks, it was a cheap education.

Ellen White offers this assurance: "Christ can give you power to overcome. By his help you can utterly destroy the root of selfishness."[6]

Service is the rent we pay for being. It is the very purpose of life, and not something you do in your spare time.
—MARION WRIGHT EDELMAN

Hang on to hope

Stop hoping and you stop living. The apostle Paul reminds us that as Christians we have evidence all around us that gives reason for hope. He writes, "Ever since the creation of the world his eternal power and divine nature, invisible though they are, have been understood and seen through the things he has made. So they are without excuse."[7]

I'm an expert hoper. Why? Because I am a Boston Red Sox fan.

Do you know how long it's been since the Boston Red Sox won the World Series? Eighty-five years! In other words, there hasn't been a baseball parade in Beantown since 1918. Think about what has happened in the world since the end of World War I. It's no wonder the Red Sox have been dubbed "the lovable losers."

As a kid growing up in Providence, Rhode Island, I would frequent Fenway Park as often as possible. I would cheer and hope—only to be disappointed again. Every year the doubters would try to drown my dreams. "It'll never happen," they'd say.

Then came 1986. At last my hopes were about to be realized. With two outs in the ninth, Mookie Wilson hit a grounder to Red Sox first baseman Bill Buckner. All he needed to do was pick up the ball and step on first base. That would have sealed a World Series title. But no, the ball rolled right through his legs—and with it, all my hopes that the curse of Boston would finally be over. That moment was almost as painful as the time Karen Tougas dumped me in second grade because Corry Carpenter offered her three Twinkies if she'd be his girlfriend instead of mine.

I'm a Red Sox fan; and not only that, I'm proud to be a Red Sox fan. I think that anybody can cheer for the Yankees. The Yankees have won twenty-six World Series titles since the Red Sox last accomplished the feat. It doesn't take much character to cheer for the Yankees. Jesus said, "If you root for the Yankees, I tell you the truth—you've had your reward in full. But to be a Red Sox fan takes character and perseverance and a steadfast spirit—and these are virtues that God will honor." OK, so I made that verse up! But it sounds like something Jesus might say, don't you think? Red Sox fans learn to hope. But really, we're all hopers. Hope is what prompts us to get back on the field and try again. Hope is the heartbeat of life.

Conversely, doubt destroys us. "Doubt," says James Allen, "has killed more splendid projects, shattered more ambitious schemes, strangled more effective geniuses, neutralized more superb efforts, blasted more fine intellects, thwarted more splendid ambitions than any other enemy of the human race."[8] Doubt is the fuel of futility.

Futility

So dare to dream. Squash the doubts that whisper:

"I'll never get into medical school."

"This world is nothing but evil."

"Jesus could never love somebody like me."

When you feed such doubts, you suffocate the soul. But hope breathes life and energy into every crevice of your character.

So hang on to hope. Even in a world wracked with war and pain we can chill in the assurance that some day soon we will be with our Father, safe at home.

This is true joy in life, the being used for a purpose recognized by yourself as a mighty one; the being thoroughly worn out before you are thrown on the scrap heap; the being a force of nature instead of a feverish selfish little clod of ailments and grievances complaining that the world will not devote itself to making you happy.

—George Bernard Shaw

Act in faith

We are called to faith—acting on a deep conviction that God knows what He's doing. Faith is the antidote to futility.

Several years ago at a prestigious university, a philosophy professor gave his students one question for the final exam. Placing a chair on top of his desk, he challenged the class by saying, "Using what you have learned this semester, prove to me that this chair does not exist."

Most of the students wrote feverishly for the entire hour. They cited heady theories and well-known philosophers. They used complex logic and debate techniques to "prove" the chair out of existence.

One student, though, wrote his name and scribbled a two-word answer. As it turned out, he was the only student who received an "A" on the final.

All he wrote was this: "What chair?"

PILGRIM'S PROBLEMS

As it turned out, only one student could see what others failed to see—an empty desk. Similarly, Christians view the world through a different lens. By faith we see what others don't see. Also, we don't see what others see. Scripture puts it like this: "The fundamental fact of existence is that this trust in God, this faith, is the firm foundation under everything that makes life worth living. It's our handle on what we can't see."[9]

So what is it that you can't see? Perhaps you can't see yourself as a great leader for God. Or you can't see yourself as being forgiven after your titanic blunder. Or you can't see God making good on His promises.

What every man needs, regardless of his job or the kind of work he is doing, is a vision of what his place is and may be. He needs an objective and a purpose. He needs a feeling and a belief that he has some worthwhile thing to do. What this is no one can tell him. It must be his own creation. Its success will be measured by the nature of his vision, what he has done to equip himself, and how well he has performed along the line of its development.

—Joseph M. Dodge

If you struggle to view life through the lens of faith rather than futility, relax. You're in good company. Moses stuttered excuses, but God made him into a great leader anyway. Peter messed up in spectacular style, but Jesus accepted him back. And Sarah laughed in God's face when He promised her a child, only to laugh more when she delivered at the ripe old age of ninety.

Like the troubled pilgrims of old, we too can enter into an adventure with God and live by faith. Faith means seeing God in all circumstances. It means trusting in Him enough to do what He calls you to do—regardless of the consequences. It's the inner conviction that God's way is the best way.

And in the end, only those who exercise faith will pass the final exam.

Futility

BRINGING IT HOME

What is the purpose of my life?

What roadblocks do I encounter in fully trusting God?

What causes my doubts?

What is my definition of hope?

Do I believe in absolute truth? If so, what beliefs would I include in this category?

Write out your worldview.

List the things that fill your life with purpose.

Ask a mature Christian to describe his/her calling in life.

Read the biography of somebody who lived on purpose.

---

[1] Ann Herbert, as adapted from <http://www.ctconfucc.org/resources/theology/beginning.html> and <http://members.rogers.com/stansgar/sermon-991031.html>.

[2] Jody and Dan Mayhew, "Submitting together," *House2House,* 2001, issue 4, 27, 28.

[3] Psalm 25:4, 5

[4] As quoted from <http://www.barna.org/cgi-binPagePressRelease.asp?PressReleaseID=106&Reference=E&Key=moral%20absolutes>.

[5] Acts 20:35.

[6] Ellen White, *Youth Instructor,* April 9, 1903, p.1.

[7] Romans 1:20, NRSV.

[8] As quoted at <http://inspirationpeak.com>.

[9] Hebrews 11:1, *The Message.*

Conclusion
A Running Commentary

"Enjoy the blessings of this day, if God sends them;
and the evils of it bear patiently and sweetly:
for this day only is ours, we are dead to yesterday,
and we are not yet born to the morrow."
—JEREMY TAYLOR

We have explored the path that all pilgrims must travel. Along the way, we have peeked inside the potholes that scar the landscape. Our problems notwithstanding, the journey is a fast one. Before you know it, life is a mural of memories. So while you still have today, squeeze the most out of life. Seize the opportunity before it's too late. Open your eyes to the wonders that dwarf the mountains you're called to climb. Sure, life is pitted with problems, but there is still reason to celebrate. Don't squander a second. Life is too worthwhile.

Recently I got a reminder to do this myself. After giving a funeral sermon for a woman who died just a few weeks before her fifty-second wedding anniversary, I stood by the casket as friends and family filed by. The last person in line was her husband. The sanctuary was empty and I wondered if perhaps I should allow him to bid farewell alone. While I didn't want to violate his privacy, I did want to show support.

I stayed, dropping my glance to their hands. His hand, polka-dotted with age spots, firmly clasped her hand, which appeared whitewashed with all the wrinkles stretched out.

Through a shower curtain of tears I stared at their hands. In my mind, I replayed the stories he had shared with me in preparation for the service. I pictured the first time they held hands at a barn party in Idaho. "I was awestruck by her beauty," he had told me. "When I asked

Conclusion

her to dance, I was so nervous I was sweating through my pants. But when I took her hand in my sweaty palm, it was like we had known each other all our lives. We twirled around that dance floor 'til three in the morning. I knew that night I had found my soulmate."

Then I pictured them at the front of the church, holding hands before sliding a gold band on each other's finger and vowing, "Till death do us part."

I pictured them in the hospital at the birth of their first child. Clutching her hand, no doubt he whispered words of support. "You're almost there, sweetheart, and we'll have a beautiful baby. Hang in there, honey." In the years that followed, their hands sandwiched tiny hands. At first they were separated by two hands, then four, then six. It wasn't long and there were four, then two. Soon the kids were gone and their hands were reunited.

Then I pictured their hands—shivering in the early stages of Parkinson's disease—clutching a knife to cut their fiftieth-wedding-anniversary cake.

I pictured their hands in more recent months as he faithfully rubbed her hands and feet every morning and evening as she courageously battled cancer. The doctor suggested the regular massages would stimulate her circulation. But with time, the disease chewed away her life, and now he was back at the altar holding her hand for the last time.

In that moment he looked up at me and whispered, "It seems like yesterday that we were twirling on the dance floor at the barn party. In a wink, it's over."

He's right. The journey is over in a heartbeat and we're left to wonder, *Where did it all go?*

Fellow pilgrim, stay strong. Lean fully on God. Put your problems in perspective. Revel in the joy of the journey because it doesn't last very long. Keep running.

That's the advice Meribeth Ditmars would leave with us. She's a teacher in Pensacola, Florida, who took up running as a way of coping with her problems. In 1997 she learned that her middle child, Christopher, had leukemia. Her life became a grueling and seemingly endless battle.

During Chris's months of chemotherapy, Meribeth said she ran loops around the hospital at dawn, looking for the endorphins that would give her the courage to face yet another day of watching her child suffer.

She ran to stay strong, hoping she could transfer her strength to Chris. Some days, it seemed to work. Chris would tease the nurses with Silly String and fake rubber vomit. He was the hospital comedian. But other days were filled with bone-wracking pain. The best they could hope for on those days was the relief of sleep.

As the treatment continued, Meribeth recruited nurses as running mates. They served as therapists on the run, listening with kindness and sympathy.

Then Meribeth discovered Team in Training, the world's largest endurance sports training program. The team provides coaches to help runners train for a marathon. In return, participants raise money for cancer research. Meribeth had never run a marathon before, but figured she could do it for Chris.

So she became a marathoner, and finished the Dublin City Marathon in 1998. Meanwhile, a miracle: Chris's disease went into remission. The leukemia was gone! Life was normal again. Meribeth was back at home running with her longtime training partner, Lorraine.

"I don't know how you keep running through all this," Lorraine would say.

"I run *because* of all this," Meribeth replied.

Listen now to Meribeth tell her story:

> When it all came crashing down again, at least I had my running. In February 2000, my 12-year-old Chris developed a tumor. We were all tested to see if we matched him for a bone marrow transplant, but no luck. So the doctors opted for more chemotherapy. This time the treatment was even longer and more aggressive. We resumed our twilight existence between two worlds: a week in the hospital, a week at home (if we were lucky).
>
> To match the intensity of Chris's treatments, I ran harder. I would run, and cry, and pray as the sun rose above the sailboats along the St. Petersburg, Florida waterfront. I thought God would listen better if I were out of breath when I called for help.[1]

Chris kept his indomitable spirit. The practical jokes and laughter never waned in his room. Chris emerged as a local hero. He landed appearances on TV and at cancer fundraisers. He talked of hope for better days ahead. Meribeth recalls that Chris put a cute, freckled cover on cancer—and once again gained remission.